MAUI TRAVEL GUIDE 2023

Everything you should know about visiting Maui including when to go, what to eat, where to stay and every other needed information

Sarah K. Cox

TABLE OF CONTENT

Welcome to Maui

Introduction to Maui

      Climate and geography of Maui

      The people of Maui

      Maui's weather

      Why should you visit Maui?

      The best season to visit Maui

Chapter 1: Historical places in Maui

      National Park Haleakala

      Iao Valley State Park

      The Historic Trail of Lahaina

      Banyan Court in Lahaina

      The Historic Trail of Kaanapali

      Kealia Pond National Wildlife Refuge

      Hana Cultural and Historical Center

      The Wailuku Historic Trail

      Sugar Museum of Alexander and Baldwin

      Jodo Mission in Lahaina

Chapter 2: Museums and Art galleries

      The Bailey House Museum

      Hui No'eau Visual Arts Center

The Maui Arts and Cultural Center

The Lahaina Arts Society

The Wo Hing Museum

Lahaina Restoration Foundation

The Maui Historical Society

International Gallery Schaefer

Hands of Maui

Viewpoints Gallery

Chapter 3: What to know before traveling

Maui requirements for entry

Travel insurance to Maui

Vaccination requirements

Downloading Maui's offline map

Different Maui common phrases

Money and tipping in Maui

Health and safety

Chapter 4: Cuisine and wine in Maui

Traditional dishes in Maui

The top ten traditional Maui dishes

Wines in Maui

The top ten wines in Maui

Restaurants on Maui that are highly recommended

Chapter 5: Activities and entertainment
Sports
Beaches
Hiking
Markets
Shopping
Souvenirs
Nightlife
Natural attractions
Maui's festivals

Chapter 6: Itenararies
What to do in 48 hours in Maui
What to do in Maui in a week

Chapter 7: Accommodation and transportation in Maui
Top hotels in Maui
Convenient mode of transportation in Maui
How to use the Maui transportation system

Chapter 8: Packing list

Packing list for females

Maui money-saving ideas

Maui time-saving advice

Maui stress-reduction strategies

Maui tourist do's and don'ts

Maui safety recommendation

Chapter 9: Understanding foreign transaction fees in Maui

Avoid phone roaming charges

Utilization of the Maui mifi device and SIM card

Maui etiquette and customs

Making new friends on Maui

Chapter 10: Travelling with family in Maui

Holiday activities for family in Maui

Traveling with children to Maui

Top Maui family activities

Children's safety in Maui

Frequently Asked Questions

Conclusion

Welcome to Maui

I recently visited Maui, and it was an unforgettable experience. Exploring the natural wonders of Maui was one of the highlights of my trip. The Haleakala National Park, which is home to the 10,000-foot-tall Haleakala Volcano, was one of the most impressive sights. We awoke early one morning to see the sunrise from the volcano's summit, and it was truly breathtaking. As the sun rose above the horizon, the sky became a rainbow of colors ranging from pink and orange to purple and blue. The vast expanse of the crater and the surrounding mountains, covered in lush vegetation, were visible as the sun's rays spread across the landscape. It was an extraordinary experience that I will never forget.

The Road to Hana was another breathtaking natural wonder. This scenic drive follows Maui's winding coastline, past lush forests, waterfalls, and breathtaking ocean views. We made several stops along the way, including Waianapanapa State Park, which has a black sand beach. The sand's color comes from volcanic rock that has been ground down over time, resulting in a one-of-a-kind and beautiful sight.

Of course, no trip to Maui would be complete without a stop at one of the island's beaches. One of my favorites was the three-mile-long Kaanapali Beach on the island's west coast. The beach is lined with luxurious resorts, restaurants, and shops, and it's a popular swimming, snorkeling, and sunbathing spot. We were fortunate to see some sea turtles while we were there, and the water is crystal clear and ideal for swimming.

Makena Beach, known for its soft, white sand and turquoise water, was another fantastic beach. It's a great place for snorkeling and swimming, and there are several nearby restaurants and cafes where you can eat. We also took a walk along the beach at sunset, watching the sky change from orange to pink to purple as the sunset.

Maui is rich in culture and history, in addition to natural beauty. The Lahaina Historic District was one of the most intriguing places we visited. This charming town is home to several historic structures, including the Lahaina Courthouse, which was once Hawaii's seat of government. We also went to the Baldwin Home Museum, which was built in 1834 and depicts life in Maui during the nineteenth century.

Attending a traditional Hawaiian luau was another fascinating cultural experience. The Luau is a festive gathering that includes traditional food, music, and dance. We dined on a delectable buffet of Hawaiian dishes such as poi (a traditional taro root dish), kalua pig (slow-roasted pork), and haupia (a coconut pudding). We also saw hula dancing, a traditional Hawaiian dance that tells stories with graceful movements and gestures.

My trip to Maui was a once-in-a-lifetime opportunity. There was something for everyone to enjoy, from the stunning natural beauty to the rich culture and history. Maui is a must-see destination for anyone looking to relax on the beach or explore the island's many wonders.

Introduction to Maui

Maui is a Hawaiian archipelago island in the central Pacific. Maui is a popular destination for travelers from all over the world due to its natural beauty. The island's stunning beaches, lush rainforests, and towering volcanoes all provide visitors with a variety of outdoor activities and adventures.

Maui, after Hawaii, is the second-largest island in the Hawaiian chain. It has a population of about 167,000 people and an area of about 727 square miles. The island is divided into five distinct regions, each of which has its distinct personality and attractions.

Some of Maui's most popular beaches can be found in the West Maui region, including Kaanapali Beach and Kapalua Beach. This area is also well-known for its luxurious resorts, golf courses, and shopping malls. The famous Road to Hana winds along the coastline past stunning waterfalls, lush forests, and picturesque beaches in the South Maui region. The Upcountry region is known for its farms, ranches, and small towns, and is located on the slopes of Haleakala Volcano. The North Shore is well-known for its surfing and windsurfing, with winter waves reaching up to 50 feet in height. Finally, the lush and remote Hana area of East Maui is known for its stunning natural beauty and cultural heritage.

Maui has a long history and culture that is deeply rooted in Hawaiian traditions. Polynesians first settled on the island about 1,500 years ago, and the Hawaiian language and culture thrived for centuries until European explorers arrived in the 18th century. Visitors to Maui can now immerse themselves in the island's rich culture and heritage through a variety of cultural activities and events, such as traditional Hawaiian luaus, hula dancing performances, and tours of historic sites and museums.

Maui is also well-known for its diverse wildlife, both on land and at sea. Several endangered species live on the island, including the Hawaiian green sea turtle, humpback whale, and Hawaiian monk seal. Maui's natural beauty and wildlife can be explored through a variety of outdoor activities, including snorkeling, scuba diving, hiking, and whale watching.

Maui has a warm and tropical climate, with temperatures ranging from the mid-70s to the mid-80s all year. The weather on the island can be unpredictable, with frequent rain showers and storms. The winter months, from December to March, are ideal for visiting Maui because the weather is cooler and the waves are larger, making it a popular time for surfers and windsurfers.

Climate and geography of Maui

The island has a tropical climate with high humidity and abundant rainfall. Several factors influence the island's climate, including its location in the Pacific Ocean, proximity to the equator, and prevailing trade winds.

Maui has a diverse landscape, with rugged mountains, lush rainforests, and pristine beaches. The island is formed by two shield volcanoes, the West Maui Mountains and Haleakala, linked by a narrow isthmus. The island is 727 square miles in size and has a 120-mile coastline.

Maui's climate is warm and tropical, with year-round temperatures ranging from the mid-70s to the mid-80s. The island is in the subtropical zone, so it gets a lot of suns and has a lot of humidity. The northeast trade winds help to moderate the temperature and provide a refreshing breeze.

The climate of Maui is influenced by the island's location in the Pacific Ocean, which means that the island experiences frequent rain showers and storms. The wettest months on the island are December to March, and the driest months are May to September. The weather, on the other hand, can be unpredictable, with sudden rain showers and temperature changes.

The West Maui Mountains and Haleakala, which are connected by a narrow isthmus, dominate the geography of Maui. The West Maui Mountains, which rise to 5,800 feet in elevation, are located in the northwest part of the island. The mountains are home to lush rainforests, waterfalls, and steep valleys that provide an incredible backdrop to Maui's west coast.

Haleakala, which means "House of the Sun" in Hawaiian, is one of the world's largest dormant volcanoes. Haleakala's summit rises to 10,023 feet in elevation and provides panoramic views of the island and surrounding ocean. The mountain also has a distinct ecosystem that supports several rare and endangered plant and animal species.

From the white sands of Kaanapali Beach in the west to the black sands of Waianapanapa Beach in the east, Maui's coastline is dotted with beautiful beaches. Tourists flock to the island's beaches, which provide a variety of activities ranging from swimming and snorkeling to surfing and windsurfing.

The interior of the island contains several small towns and villages, as well as vast tracts of undeveloped land used for farming, ranching, and conservation. The Upcountry region, located on Haleakala's slopes, is known for its scenic beauty, small towns, and farms that produce a variety of fruits, vegetables, and flowers. Several popular attractions in the area include the Haleakala Crater and the Maui Winery.

The people of Maui

Maui's people are a diverse group with distinct cultural backgrounds and traditions. They are descended from Polynesians who first arrived on the island around 1,500 years ago.

Maui is known for its warm hospitality and welcoming nature. They are ecstatic to share their culture and heritage with visitors. The island's economy is heavily reliant on tourism, and the locals are eager to give visitors a true Hawaiian experience.

Hula is a prominent cultural tradition of the Maui people. Hula is a traditional Hawaiian dance that uses movement and song to tell a story. It is a way for the people of Maui to honor their ancestors and connect with their past. Hula is frequently performed at festivals and celebrations, and visitors to Maui can see hula shows or even take hula lessons.

Another important aspect of Maui culture is the people's connection to the land and sea. Beautiful beaches, lush forests, and breathtaking mountains surround the island. The locals are extremely proud of their natural surroundings and are committed to environmental preservation. Many Maui residents participate in eco-tourism and work to protect the island's vulnerable ecosystems.

Maui's people are also very proud of their ancestors and their history. The island is home to several historic sites and museums that highlight Maui's rich cultural heritage. The Haleakala National Park is a popular destination for Maui visitors, and it contains many significant cultural and historical sites, such as ancient Hawaiian temples and burial sites.

Maui residents are also known for their love of food. The cuisine on the island is a fusion of Polynesian, Asian, and American influences, with local dishes reflecting the island's diverse cultural heritage. Poke, a raw fish salad, and loco moco, a dish made of rice, a hamburger patty, and gravy, are two of the most popular foods on the island.

Maui's people are deeply spiritual, and religion is an important part of their daily lives. Many residents follow the traditional Hawaiian religion, which is based on a belief in a spiritual force known as mana. Mana is thought to circulate through all living things and is necessary for healing and spiritual development.

Aside from traditional Hawaiian religion, the island is home to a variety of other religious traditions. Maui has a large number of Christian churches,

Buddhist temples, and synagogues, and the people of Maui are open to and respectful of all religions.

Maui's weather

The weather in Maui is a major factor that draws visitors all year. The island's location in the Central Pacific Ocean, combined with its varied topography, results in a distinct and diverse climate that varies greatly depending on location and season. Maui has a tropical climate, with warm temperatures, plenty of sunshine, and only a little rain.

Summer and winter are the two main seasons in Maui. Summer lasts from May to October, and winter lasts from November to April. During the summer, temperatures on Maui average in the mid-80s°F (30°C) during the day and drop to the mid-60s°F (18°C) at night. The humidity level is also relatively high at this time of year, with occasional trade winds providing some relief.

Maui experiences cooler temperatures and more rainfall during the winter, particularly in the island's higher elevations. During the winter months, the average temperature ranges from the mid-70s°F (23°C) during the day to the low 60s°F (16°C) at night. During the winter months, the trade winds are also stronger, providing relief from the humidity and aiding in the cooling of the island.

The climate in Maui varies greatly depending on location. The topography of the island is varied, with high mountains, coastal plains, and valleys. The island's western and southern coasts are generally drier and sunnier, while the island's eastern and northern coasts receive more rain. The interior of the island, with its lush forests and waterfalls, is also cooler and wetter.

The trade winds are a notable weather phenomenon in Maui. These northeast winds are a constant presence on the island. During the summer, trade winds provide relief from the heat and humidity, whereas in the winter, they can be stronger, bringing cooler temperatures and more rainfall.

The Kona winds are another weather feature that impacts Maui. The southwest winds are warm and humid. They can bring vog (volcanic smog) from the Big Island, which can have an impact on Maui's air quality. During the winter, Kona winds can bring heavy rain and storms.

The weather in Maui is also important to the island's agriculture. Many farms and orchards are located on the island, including pineapple, coffee, and macadamia nut farms. The tropical climate and abundant rainfall make these crops ideal for growing, and visitors can tour the farms and sample the fresh produce.

Why should you visit Maui?

Maui is a beautiful place to visit, as previously stated. Here are some of the reasons why you should go to Maui.

Gorgeous beaches

Maui is home to some of the world's most beautiful beaches. Maui has beaches for everyone, whether you want to relax or surf. Kaanapali Beach, known for its clear waters and soft sand, and Makena Beach, a secluded spot with excellent snorkeling opportunities, are two of the most popular beaches on the island.

Natural beauty at its best

The natural splendor of Maui is breathtaking. Lush forests, towering mountains, and breathtaking waterfalls can be found on the island. The Road to

Hana, a scenic drive that winds through lush forests and past cascading waterfalls, is one of the most popular natural attractions on the island. The Haleakala National Park, which is home to the dormant Haleakala volcano and offers breathtaking views of the island from its summit, is another must-see natural attraction.

A wealth of cultural heritage

Maui has a thriving cultural heritage that is celebrated all over the island. The residents of the island are proud of their Polynesian ancestry and eager to share it with visitors. Visitors can enjoy traditional Hawaiian music and dance, as well as learn about the island's history at local museums and restaurants.

Activities that take place outside

Outdoor enthusiasts will love Maui. Surfing, snorkeling, scuba diving, hiking, and zip-lining are among the many activities available to visitors. The island's warm, sunny climate makes it ideal for outdoor activities all year.

Eco-tourism

Maui is dedicated to environmental preservation and ecotourism. Eco-tours that focus on preserving the island's unique ecosystems are available to visitors. Whale-watching tours, bird-watching tours, and hikes through the island's lush forests are among the eco-tourism activities available.

The delicious cuisine

The cuisine of Maui is a synthesis of Polynesian, Asian, and American influences. Poi (a traditional Hawaiian staple made from taro), laulau (a dish made from pork and fish wrapped in taro leaves), and poke are among the traditional Hawaiian foods available to visitors (a raw fish salad). Maui also has several fine dining establishments that serve fresh, local ingredients as well as a variety of international cuisine.

Friendly locals

Maui's people are known for their friendly nature and warm hospitality. Visitors are frequently struck by the welcoming attitude of the locals, who are eager to share their island with visitors. The people of the island are proud of their home and eager to show visitors everything it has to offer.

Romance

Maui is a popular romantic vacation destination for couples. The island's stunning natural beauty and warm climate are ideal for a romantic getaway. On the island, numerous luxury resorts offer couples' packages and romantic activities such as sunset dinners and couples' massages.

The best season to visit Maui

The weather is more pleasant for tourists at certain times of the year. We'll talk about the best time to visit Maui in this guide.

Maui is best visited between April and May, and between September and November. The island experiences milder temperatures, fewer crowds, and lower lodging prices during these months. During these months, the weather is also generally dryer, making it ideal for outdoor activities such as hiking, snorkeling, and surfing.

Spring (April to May)

Spring is regarded as one of the best seasons for visiting Maui. The temperature ranges from 75°F (24°C) to 85°F (29°C). The island is less crowded at this time of year, making it ideal for outdoor activities. Humpback whales migrate to the warm waters around Maui in the spring to mate and give birth to their calves. Visitors can witness these majestic creatures up close by taking a whale-watching tour.

Summer (June to August)

Summer is the busiest tourist season in Maui, with the highest crowds and lodging prices. Temperatures range from 85°F (29°C) to 90°F (32°C). Visitors should expect rain showers and high humidity. The island's beautiful beaches and warm waters, on the other hand, make it an excellent time for swimming, snorkeling, and surfing.

Fall (September to November)

Another excellent time to visit Maui is in the fall. The temperature ranges from 75°F (24°C) to 85°F (29°C). The island is less crowded at this time of year, making it ideal for outdoor activities like hiking, snorkeling, and surfing. The island also celebrates its cultural heritage during the fall season, with several festivals and events.

Winter (December to March)

The rainy season in Maui is winter, and the island receives the most rainfall during this time of year. The temperature ranges from 70°F (21°C) to 80°F (27°C). The humidity on the island is higher, and visitors can expect rain showers on occasion. However, winter is also the season for big wave surfing, and visitors can watch some of the world's best surfers take on the island's north shore's massive waves.

Chapter 1: Historical places in Maui

Maui is not only a beautiful island destination, but it is also historically and culturally significant. There are numerous historical sites to visit on the island, ranging from ancient Hawaiian temples to historic landmarks. In this guide, we'll look at some of the most important historical sites on Maui, as well as how to get there.

• National Park Haleakala

Haleakala National Park is a popular tourist destination in Maui that is also rich in history. The park is home to the massive volcanic crater Haleakala Crater, which is over 7 miles long and 2 miles wide. The crater is considered sacred by native Hawaiians and is said to be the residence of the demigod Maui.

Visitors can hike the park's numerous trails and enjoy breathtaking views of the crater and surrounding landscape. Visitors can reach the park by taking the Haleakala Highway from Kahului. The drive takes about 1.5 hours, and several lookout points along the way provide breathtaking views of the island.

• Iao Valley State Park

Another historical attraction on Maui is Iao Valley State Park. The Iao Needle, a 1,200-foot-tall rock formation, is located within the park. The ancient Hawaiians used the needle as a navigational landmark, and it is considered a sacred site.

Visitors can hike the park's trails and enjoy the stunning scenery, which includes numerous waterfalls and streams. Visitors can reach Iao Valley State Park by taking the Honoapiilani Highway from Lahaina. The drive takes about 30 minutes, and there is plenty of parking at the park.

• The Historic Trail of Lahaina

The Lahaina Historic Trail is a self-guided walking tour through Lahaina's historic district. The trail includes 62 historical sites such as churches, museums, and landmarks. Visitors can learn about the town's rich history, from its days as a whaling village to its current role as the Kingdom of Hawaii's capital.

Visitors can reach the Lahaina Historic Trail by taking the Honoapiilani Highway from Kahului.

The drive takes about 45 minutes, and there is plenty of parking in Lahaina.

● Banyan Court in Lahaina

Lahaina Banyan Court is a public park in the center of Lahaina. One of the largest banyan trees in the United States can be found in the park, which was planted in 1873 to commemorate the 50th anniversary of the arrival of the first American missionaries in Hawaii.

Visitors can enjoy the massive tree's beauty while also exploring the park's many walking paths and benches. Visitors can take the Honoapiilani Highway from Kahului to get to the Lahaina Banyan Court. The drive takes about 45 minutes, and there is plenty of parking in Lahaina.

- **The Historic Trail of Kaanapali**

Another self-guided walking tour that takes visitors through the historic town of Kaanapali is the Kaanapali Historic Trail. The trail includes ten different historical sites, including the remains of ancient Hawaiian temples and plantation landmarks.

Visitors can take the Honoapiilani Highway from Kahului to reach the Kaanapali Historic Trail. The drive takes about 45 minutes, and there is plenty of parking in Kaanapali.

- **Kealia Pond National Wildlife Refuge**

Kealia Pond National Wildlife Refuge is a wetland reserve where many native Hawaiian bird species can be found. The refuge is also a significant site for ancient Hawaiian salt-making, with remnants of ancient salt pans visible on the trail. Visitors can reach the refuge by taking the Mokulele Highway from Kahului. The drive takes about 20 minutes, and there is plenty of parking at the refuge.

• Hana Cultural and Historical Center

The Hana Cultural Center and Museum highlight the town 's history and culture, including artifacts and exhibits that highlight the area's ancient Hawaiian heritage. Visitors can take the Hana Highway from Kahului to Hana. The drive takes about 2-3 hours, depending on traffic, and provides breathtaking views of the island's coastline and tropical rainforests.

• The Wailuku Historic Trail

The Wailuku Historic Trail is a self-guided walking tour that takes visitors through Wailuku's historic district. The trail includes 19 different historical sites that highlight the town's rich history, such as museums, churches, and landmarks. Visitors can take Kaahumanu Avenue from Kahului to Wailuku. The drive takes about 10 minutes, and there is plenty of parking in town.

• Sugar Museum of Alexander and Baldwin

The Alexander & Baldwin Sugar Museum commemorates Maui's sugar cultivation history, with exhibits on the island's plantation days and the impact of the sugar industry on the local community. Visitors can reach the museum by taking the Honoapiilani Highway from Kahului. The drive takes about 20 minutes, and there is plenty of parking at the museum.

• Jodo Mission in Lahaina

The Lahaina Jodo Mission is a Buddhist temple founded in 1912. The temple has a large bronze Buddha statue and lovely Japanese gardens, which provide visitors with a peaceful and tranquil escape. Visitors can reach the temple by taking the Honoapiilani Highway from Kahului. The drive takes about 45 minutes, and there is plenty of parking at the temple.

Chapter 2: Museums and Art galleries

Maui is not only a lovely tropical island with beaches and outdoor activities, but it is also a cultural and artistic hotspot. Several museums and art galleries on the island showcase Hawaii's rich history and culture. Here are ten Maui museums and art galleries to visit, along with directions:

• The Bailey House Museum

The Bailey House Museum is a historic house in Wailuku that has been converted into a museum. It houses a large collection of Hawaiian artifacts and exhibits that tell the history and culture of the island. Visitors can take Kaahumanu Avenue from Kahului, which takes approximately 10-15 minutes.

- **Hui No'eau Visual Arts Center**

The Hui No'eau Visual Arts Center in Makawao hosts a variety of art exhibitions, classes, and workshops. The center, which is housed in a historic plantation estate, has several galleries and studios. Visitors can take the Haleakala Highway from Kahului, which takes approximately 20-25 minutes.

- **The Maui Arts and Cultural Center**

The Maui Arts & Cultural Center, located in Kahului, is the largest performing arts venue on the island. It has several theaters, galleries, and classrooms where local and international artists, performers, and events are showcased. Visitors can get there by taking the Kaahumanu Avenue from Kahului, which takes about 5-10 minutes.

• The Lahaina Arts Society

The Lahaina Arts Society is a charitable organization that promotes and supports local artists. It has a gallery as well as art fairs where you can see paintings, sculptures, and jewelry. Visitors can take the Honoapiilani Highway from Kahului, which takes approximately 45-50 minutes.

• The Wo Hing Museum

The Wo Hing Museum in Lahaina tells the story of Chinese immigrants who arrived in Maui in the nineteenth century. Artifacts, photographs, and antiques are among the exhibits at the museum that highlights the island's Chinese heritage. Visitors can take the Honoapiilani Highway from Kahului, which takes approximately 45-50 minutes.

• Lahaina Restoration Foundation

The Lahaina Restoration Foundation is a non-profit organization dedicated to preserving and promoting the historic and cultural significance of the town of Lahaina. It is home to several museums, including the Baldwin Home Museum, the Old Lahaina Courthouse, and the Plantation Museum. Visitors can take the Honoapiilani Highway from Kahului, which takes approximately 45-50 minutes.

• The Maui Historical Society

The Maui Historical Society, located in Wailuku, has a museum and a research library that showcase the history and culture of the island. The museum houses a variety of exhibits, including photographs, documents, and artifacts dating back to the island's early days. Visitors can take Kaahumanu Avenue from Kahului, which takes approximately 10-15 minutes.

• International Gallery Schaefer

The Schaefer International Gallery, which is part of the Maui Arts & Cultural Center, hosts a variety of international art exhibitions. It houses several galleries that display contemporary and modern artworks such as paintings, sculptures, and installations. Visitors can get there by taking the Kaahumanu Avenue from Kahului, which takes about 5-10 minutes.

• Hands of Maui

Maui Hands is a gallery that showcases a wide range of art and crafts created by local artists. It displays a variety of artworks, including paintings, ceramics, glasswork, and jewelry. It has several locations on the island, including Paia, Lahaina, and Makawao, so visitors can choose the most convenient location for them.

• Viewpoints Gallery

Viewpoints Gallery in Makawao houses a collection of fine art, jewelry, and crafts created by local artists. The gallery has a warm, inviting atmosphere that makes visitors feel at ease. Visitors can take the Haleakala Highway from Kahului, which takes approximately 20-25 minutes.

Visitors can also visit the Maui Arts & Cultural Center's Schaefer International Gallery, which hosts many international art exhibitions featuring contemporary and modern artworks such as paintings, sculptures, and installations.

Chapter 3: What to know before traveling

Traveling to a new place can be exciting, but it's always a good idea to be prepared and informed. Here are some things you should know before visiting Maui:

Travel documents: Before your trip, make sure you have a valid passport and any necessary visas or travel documents. It is also advisable to keep copies of these documents in a secure location, such as a hotel safe or digital storage.

Weather: Maui has a tropical climate, so it can be hot and humid all year. Pack lightweight, breathable clothing. Remember that Maui has a rainy season from November to March, so bring rain gear.

Time difference: Due to daylight savings time, Maui is 2-3 hours behind the West Coast of the United States. Visitors should make necessary adjustments to their schedules.

Currency: The US dollar is the currency in Maui. Credit cards are widely accepted, but having some cash on hand for small purchases and tips is a good idea.

Transportation: Transportation in Maui includes rental cars, taxis, ride-sharing services, and public transportation. To avoid last-minute problems, it is critical to conduct advanced research and planning on transportation options.

Activities: Hiking, snorkeling, and visiting cultural and historical sites are just a few of the outdoor activities and attractions on Maui. To make the most of your trip and ensure availability for popular activities and attractions, it is critical to research and plans ahead of time.

Custom and etiquette: Visitors should be respectful of local customs and etiquette. Before entering a home, temple, or another sacred place, remove your shoes. Visitors should also be mindful of local wildlife and ecosystems, adhering to the principles of Leave No Trace.

Maui requirements for entry

The United States government determines the entry requirements for visitors to Maui, which may differ depending on the traveler's country of origin. Here are some important Maui entry requirements to be aware of:

Visa requirements: Many countries' citizens are eligible to travel to the United States under the Visa Waiver Program, which allows them to stay in the country for up to 90 days without a visa. Travelers must have an electronic passport, also known as an e-passport, to participate in the Visa Waiver

Program. Citizens of non-Visa Waiver Program countries must obtain a visa before traveling to the United States.

Before traveling to the United States, travelers who are eligible for the Visa Waiver Program must also obtain Electronic System for Travel Authorization (ESTA) authorization. The Electronic System for Travel Authorization (ESTA) is an automated system that determines whether visitors are eligible to travel to the United States under the Visa Waiver Program. ESTA authorization is available online and must be obtained at least 72 hours before departure.

COVID-19 restrictions: Due to the COVID-19 pandemic, visitors to the United States, including Maui, may face additional entry requirements and restrictions. Currently, all travelers must show proof of a negative COVID-19 test taken no more than three days before departure, regardless of vaccination status. Depending on their vaccination status and other factors, travelers may also be required to quarantine upon arrival.

Customs declaration: Before entering the United States, all visitors must fill out a customs declaration form. The form requests information about the traveler's trip, such as the purpose of the visit, countries visited before arriving in the United States, and items brought into the country.

Health: While no specific health requirements exist for visiting Maui, visitors should be aware of potential health risks and take appropriate precautions. The island is home to several endemic diseases, including dengue fever and rat lungworm disease, which are spread by mosquitoes and snails, respectively. Visitors should use insect repellent and wear long sleeves and pants to protect themselves against mosquito and snail bites.

Travel insurance to Maui

Travel insurance can give visitors to Maui peace of mind by protecting them from unexpected events that could disrupt or cancel their trip. Here are some essential Maui travel insurance facts:

Travel insurance policies: can provide coverage for a variety of events, including trip cancellations or interruptions, medical emergencies, lost or stolen luggage, and travel delays. Some policies may also cover activities like snorkeling and hiking.

The cost of coverage: This varies depending on the level of coverage, the length of the trip, the age and health of the traveler, and other factors. Policies with higher coverage limits and more comprehensive coverage will generally be more expensive.

Considerations for Maui: It is critical to consider the activities and risks associated with the destination when selecting a travel insurance policy for Maui. Travelers who intend to participate in water activities such as snorkeling or surfing, for example, should look for policies that specifically cover those activities.

Exclusions for pre-existing medical conditions: are common in many travel insurance policies, making it difficult for travelers with chronic health issues to find suitable coverage. Some policies may cover pre-existing conditions if purchased within a certain time frame of booking the trip.

Medical coverage for emergencies: Medical care in Maui can be costly for visitors, especially in the event of a medical emergency. Travel insurance policies can include emergency medical treatment and evacuation coverage, which can help protect against unexpected medical costs.

Trip cancellation/interruption coverage: Travelers who are forced to cancel or shorten their trip due to unforeseen circumstances such as a medical emergency or natural disaster may be able to recoup some or all of their trip costs with travel insurance.

Coverage limits and deductibles: Coverage limits and deductibles in travel insurance policies can affect how much protection a traveler receives and how much they will have to pay out of pocket if they file a claim. Before purchasing, carefully review the policy's coverage limits and deductibles.

Vaccination requirements

All visitors to Maui must be fully vaccinated against COVID-19 by September 2021, or provide proof of a negative COVID-19 test result obtained within 72 hours of departure. Before flying to Maui, visitors must show proof of vaccination or a negative test result.

Other vaccinations are recommended for visitors to Maui, in addition to the COVID-19 vaccination. Among these are:

Hepatitis A: is a contagious liver disease spread by contaminated food and water. Visitors who plan to eat at local restaurants or engage in outdoor activities such as hiking or camping may be more susceptible to hepatitis A. All visitors to Maui should get the hepatitis A vaccine, especially if they are staying for an extended period or have a pre-existing liver condition.

Hepatitis B: Another contagious liver disease that can be transmitted through contact with infected blood or bodily fluids is hepatitis B. Travelers who intend to have sexual contact with locals, get a tattoo or piercing, or receive medical treatment on

Maui may be at a higher risk of contracting hepatitis B. All visitors to Maui should get vaccinated against hepatitis B, especially those who plan to engage in high-risk activities.

Influenza: The flu is contagious in Maui all year and can cause severe illness in some people. The influenza vaccine is recommended for all Maui visitors, particularly those who are at high risk of flu complications, such as the elderly or those with chronic medical conditions.

Mumps, rubella, and measles (MMR): The MMR vaccine is recommended for all travelers who were not vaccinated as children or who have never had the disease. Measles outbreaks have occurred in Hawaii in recent years, putting unvaccinated visitors at risk.

It's important to note that some of these vaccines require a series of doses, so visitors to Maui should plan ahead of time and get the necessary vaccinations. It is also critical to consult with a healthcare provider to determine which vaccinations are appropriate for each traveler based on their specific health and travel plans.

Downloading Maui's offline map

Step 1: Select a mapping application

The first step in downloading an offline map for Maui is to find a map app that you like. There are numerous options, but the most popular is Google Maps, Maps. me, and HERE WeGo. Each app has its own set of advantages and disadvantages, so do your homework to find the one that best meets your needs.

Google Maps is a popular app that provides detailed maps as well as real-time traffic updates. It's free and simple to use, but it requires a consistent internet connection to work properly. While a portion of the map can be downloaded for offline use, the offline maps are limited to a specific area and must be re-downloaded regularly.

Another popular app is Maps. me, which provides offline maps for over 195 countries. It's free to use and doesn't require an internet connection, but the maps aren't always as detailed as those provided by Google Maps.

HERE WeGo is a free app that provides detailed offline maps as well as traffic updates in real-time. It also lets you download maps for an entire country, which is useful if you plan on spending a lot of time on Maui.

Step 2: Get the Map

After you've decided on a map app, download the Maui map. The steps may vary slightly depending on which app you use, but the general procedure is as follows:

- Open your device's map app
- Look for the word Maui
- Select the "Download" icon or button
- Select the area to download
- Allow for the download to finish
- To ensure that the offline map works, switch your device to airplane mode

It is important to note that the size of the map you download will be determined by the app you use and the area you wish to cover. A map of the entire island of Maui, for example, will be larger than a map of just the town of Lahaina.

Step 3: Navigate using the Offline Map

You can use the map offline after you've downloaded it. Here are some tips for making the most of your offline map:

Make sure your GPS is activated: Even if you're not connected to the internet, your device can still track your location as long as your GPS is turned on.

To navigate, use landmarks: Because you won't be able to see real-time traffic updates while offline, it's critical to use landmarks to help you navigate. If you're driving to the beach, for example, look for signs or landmarks along the way, such as a hotel or restaurant.

Save locations in advance: Make a list of the places you want to visit on your offline map before you leave. This way, even if you don't have an internet connection, you'll be able to access them.

Periodically check for updates: Depending on the app, you may need to update your offline map regularly to ensure you have the most up-to-date information.

Different Maui common phrases

Visitors and residents alike appreciate the island's unique slang and common phrases. These expressions are a blend of Hawaiian and English words and expressions that have evolved to reflect the island's rich cultural heritage. This guide will look at some of the most commonly used Maui phrases and their meanings.

Aloha

"Aloha" means hello, goodbye, love, and affection in Maui. The literal translation of the word is "life's breath," and it represents the Hawaiian spirit of hospitality, kindness, and respect.

Mahalo

"Mahalo," which means "thank you" or "gratitude," is another popular Maui phrase. Locals say "mahalo" to express gratitude for a kind gesture, a delicious meal, or a stunning sunset.

E komo mai

If you're invited to a local's home or a gathering, you'll likely hear the phrase "e komo mai," which means welcome. This phrase is an invitation to join in the fun and enjoy the company of family and friends.

Pau hana

When the workday is done, the phrase "pau hana" (finished with work) is commonly heard. This phrase marks the beginning of the evening, a time to unwind and relax with friends and family.

Ono grinds

"Ono grinds" is a Maui word for delicious food. Local Hawaiian cuisines, such as poke, spam musubi, and loco moco, are frequently described using this phrase.

Pono

To do what is right or to live in balance and harmony with oneself and others is what the Maui phrase "pono" means. Pono is a guiding principle for many Hawaiians, and it is frequently linked to the concept of aloha.

Malama

Malama is a Maui word that means to care for or protect. This phrase is frequently used in the context of environmental conservation or the preservation of Maui's natural beauty.

Ohana

"Ohana" means "family" in Hawaiian. This phrase expresses the value of family and community in Hawaiian culture, and it is frequently used to describe close friends and loved ones.

Da kine

"Da kine" is a Maui phrase for something you can't quite remember or describe. This phrase has a wide range of applications and can refer to anything from a person to an object to an idea.

Talk story

When a group of locals gets together to talk and catch up, they frequently say they're going to "talk story." This Maui phrase expresses the significance of oral storytelling in Hawaiian culture and serves as an invitation to share stories and connect.

Hana hou

"Hana hou," a Maui phrase that means "do it again," means "do it again." This phrase is commonly used to encourage performers to repeat a favorite song or dance at concerts, performances, and other events.

Mauka and makai

Mauka and makai are Hawaiian terms.

The words "mauka" and "makai" are used to describe directions in Maui. "Mauka" refers to the mountains, whereas "makai" refers to the sea.

Shaka

The "shaka," or Maui hand gesture, is a popular way to greet people and demonstrate aloha spirit. Extend your thumb and pinky finger while curling your other fingers into your palm to make a shaka.

Kama'aina

"Kama'aina" is a Maui term that refers to a local or someone who has lived on the island for a long time.

Money and tipping in Maui

Money and tipping are two topics that frequently come up when discussing Maui travel. In this guide, we'll look at the significance of money and tipping in Maui, as well as some helpful hints and guidelines to keep in mind while there.

Maui money

Maui, like the rest of Hawaii, uses US dollars as its currency. While credit cards are widely accepted on the island, having some cash on hand for smaller purchases like souvenirs, snacks, or local transportation is always a good idea.

ATMs are widely available on Maui, allowing you to easily withdraw cash if necessary. However, some ATMs may charge a fee for withdrawals, so check with your bank ahead of time to see if they have any partnerships or agreements with ATMs in Hawaii.

It's best to exchange currency before arriving in Maui. While some hotels and resorts may provide currency exchange services, the exchange rates are usually not as favorable as those found at banks or exchange offices.

Tipping on Maui is customary

Tipping is an important part of the service industry in Maui, as it is across the country. Waiters, bartenders, and hotel staff rely heavily on tips as a source of income. As a result, it's critical to understand Maui's traditional tipping practices.

Restaurants and bars

It is customary to tip 15-20% of the total bill in restaurants and bars. It is important to note, however, that for larger groups, some restaurants may automatically add a gratuity to the bill. In these cases, you have the option of adding a tip on top of the already included gratuity.

It should also be noted that some Maui restaurants may include a service charge on the bill, which is not the same as a gratuity. Service charges are typically a fixed percentage of the total bill and are used to cover the restaurant's operating expenses. It is not necessary to leave an additional tip in these cases, but you may do so if you believe the service was exceptional.

Hotel and resort facilities

It is customary to tip hotel staff in Maui, such as bellhops, housekeeping staff, and concierges. A good rule of thumb is to tip housekeeping staff $2-5 per day, bellhops $1-2 per bag, and concierges $5-20 per day.

Transportation

A tip of 15-20% of the total fare is customary when using Maui transportation services such as taxis, ride-sharing services, or tour guides. However, check ahead of time to see if the fare already includes a gratuity, as some tour companies or transportation services may automatically add a gratuity to the bill.

Additional Services

Hairdressers, spa services, and massage therapists are also common tips in Maui. For these services, it is customary to leave a tip of 15-20% of the total bill.

Health and safety

While the island is generally regarded as a safe destination, there are a few health and safety precautions that visitors should be aware of. This guide will go over some of the most important health and safety precautions to take when visiting Maui.

Protection from the sun

Because of Maui's tropical climate, the sun shines brightly all year, and visitors should take precautions to shield themselves from the sun's harmful rays. Sunburns and skin damage can happen quickly, especially between 10 a.m. and 4 p.m. Visitors should avoid sunburn and skin damage by doing the following:

- Wear a high-SPF sunscreen (at least 30) and reapply it frequently throughout the day.
- When possible, put on protective clothing such as hats, long-sleeved shirts, and pants.
- During the hottest hours of the day, seek shade.
- To stay hydrated, drink plenty of water.

Water Protection

One of the main draws for visitors to Maui is the beautiful beaches and crystal-clear waters, but it's important to be aware of the potential dangers associated with water activities. Visitors are advised to:

- Swim and surf in designated areas only, and always obey posted signs and warnings.
- Be aware of the strong and dangerous tides and currents.
- When entering the water, exercise caution because there may be rocks or other hazards beneath the surface.
- When snorkeling or paddleboarding, wear a life jacket.
- When children are in or near water, they must always be supervised.

Weather Security

Hurricanes, heavy rain, and flash floods are all possible in Maui's tropical climate. Visitors are advised to:

- Weather alerts and warnings can be found on the National Weather Service website or through local news outlets.

- Prepare for unexpected weather changes, especially during hurricane season (June to November).
- In the event of an emergency, obey local authorities' instructions, including evacuation orders.

Wildlife safety

Maui's wildlife includes sea turtles, dolphins, and whales, which can be seen on boat tours and other activities. Visitors are advised to:

- Maintain a safe distance from wildlife
- Touching or feeding wildlife can be hazardous to both the animal and the visitor.
- Be aware of potential wildlife hazards such as jellyfish stings and shark sightings.

The safety of food and water

Visitors to Maui should also be aware of food and water safety concerns, such as the possibility of foodborne illness and waterborne diseases. Visitors should avoid becoming ill by doing the following:

- To avoid waterborne diseases, drink bottled or filtered water.
- They must frequently wash their hands, especially before eating or handling food.
- Select restaurants and food vendors who practice good hygiene.
- Consuming raw or undercooked seafood increases your risk of foodborne illness.

COVID-19 Protection

The COVID-19 pandemic has hit Maui, as it has many other places around the world, and visitors should take precautions to protect themselves and others from the virus. Visitors are advised to:

- As required by state law, wear a mask in public indoor settings and crowded outdoor settings.

- Keep a safe distance from other people, especially in crowded places.
- When handwashing is not an option, they should use hand sanitizer.
- If at all possible, get vaccinated against COVID-19 before traveling to Maui.
- Local authorities may impose additional guidelines or requirements.

Chapter 4: Cuisine and wine in Maui

One aspect of Maui's culture that visitors often enjoy is its cuisine and wine scene. In this guide, we will explore some of the best restaurants, dishes, and wines to try when visiting Maui.

Traditional dishes in Maui

The island's Hawaiian, Polynesian, and Asian heritage, as well as its proximity to the Pacific Ocean, all have an impact on Maui's traditional dishes. This guide will look at some of Maui's most popular traditional dishes.

Poke

Poke is a popular traditional Hawaiian dish that has grown in popularity in recent years. It is made up of bite-sized pieces of raw fish, usually ahi tuna or salmon, that have been marinated in a flavorful sauce made with soy sauce, sesame oil, and other ingredients such as green onions, chili peppers, and seaweed. Poke can be served as a starter or as a main course with rice or salad.

Pig Kalua

Kalua pig is a slow-roasted pork dish popular in Hawaii. The pig is traditionally cooked in an imu, an underground oven that uses hot rocks and banana leaves to steam the pig, imparting a smoky, flavorful flavor. After that, the meat is shredded and served with rice, macaroni salad, and other sides.

Moco Loco

A bed of white rice is topped with a hamburger patty, fried egg, and brown gravy in Loco Moco, a popular Hawaiian breakfast dish. The dish originated in Hilo, Hawaii, and has since spread throughout the islands as a popular comfort food. Adding Spam or Portuguese sausage to the patty is one variation of the dish.

Musubi made with Spam

Spam musubi is a popular Hawaiian snack that combines Japanese rice balls with Spam, a canned meat product that became popular during WWII. A slice of grilled Spam is served on top of a block of rice, wrapped in a strip of nori seaweed. It's a quick and easy on-the-go snack.

Plate Lunch

Plate lunch is a popular Hawaiian dish that consists of a protein, such as a teriyaki chicken or kalua pig, served over rice with macaroni salad and vegetables on the side. During the sugar plantation era, when workers needed a filling and affordable meal, the dish was created. Plate lunch is now a staple of Hawaiian cuisine, available at a variety of local restaurants and food trucks.

Haupia

Haupia, also known as coconut pudding in Hawaii, is a traditional Hawaiian dessert. It's typically served in small squares or molded into various shapes and is made with coconut milk, sugar, and cornstarch. Haupia is frequently served at luaus and other Hawaiian celebrations, and it can be eaten alone or as a topping for other desserts.

Malasadas

Malasadas are Portuguese donuts that have grown in popularity as Hawaiian desserts. The dough is made with yeast, flour, sugar, eggs, and butter, and it is then deep-fried until golden brown. Malasadas are often coated in sugar and filled with various fillings such as custard or chocolate.

Shaved ice

Shave ice is a cool dessert that is ideal for the hot Maui weather. It's made by shaving a block of ice and topping it with flavored syrups like pineapple or mango. Shave ice is frequently accompanied by a scoop of vanilla ice cream and sweetened condensed milk.

Laulau

Laulau is a traditional Hawaiian dish made of taro leaves wrapped around pork or fish and steamed until tender. Poi, a starchy Hawaiian staple made from taro root, is frequently served alongside the dish. Laulau is a time-consuming dish to make, but the result is a savory, tender meal that is well worth the effort.

Pipikaula

Pipikaula is a Hawaiian beef jerky that was invented to preserve meat. Before being dried and smoked, the beef is marinated in a combination of soy sauce, sugar, and other seasonings. Pipikaula is a popular Hawaiian snack that is frequently served as an appetizer at local restaurants. It can also be used as a salad or other dish topping.

The top ten traditional Maui dishes

Sure, here are the top ten Maui traditional dishes:

- Poke
- Pig Kalua
- Moco Loco
- Musubi made with Spam
- Plate Lunch
- Haupia
- Malasadas
- Ice should be shaved
- Laulau
- Pipikaula

Wines in Maui

When most people think of wine, they imagine the lush vineyards of Napa Valley or the rolling hills of

Tuscany. However, it may surprise you to learn that Maui, a Hawaiian island, has its wine industry. This guide will look at the history and production of Maui wine, as well as some of the island's most notable wineries.

The Evolution of Maui Wine

Maui wine began in the early 1970s, when two University of Hawaii professors, Dr. Hector and Mrs. Josephine Montrond, planted a vineyard on the slopes of Haleakala, Maui's dormant volcano. The couple tested various grape varieties and techniques until they discovered what worked best in Maui's unique climate and soil. Tedeschi Vineyards, Maui's first commercial winery, was founded in 1977.

Maui's wine industry has grown significantly since then, with more wineries and vineyards springing up all over the island. Maui now has several award-winning wineries producing wines ranging from crisp whites to bold reds.

Maui Wine

Maui's winemaking is unique in that it is influenced not only by the island's climate but also by its volcanic soil, which is rich in minerals and nutrients. The volcanic soil is ideal for grape cultivation because it allows for good drainage and creates a distinct mineral profile in the grapes, giving Maui wines a distinct flavor.

Maui's climate is also conducive to wine production. The warm, tropical weather and plentiful rainfall on the island make for ideal grape-growing conditions. Cooler temperatures at higher elevations on Haleakala's slopes provide an ideal climate for growing grapes such as Syrah and Malbec, which require cooler temperatures to ripen properly.

Maui Wineries

Tedeschi Vineyards

Maui's first commercial winery, Tedeschi Vineyards, is still in business today. The winery makes a variety of wines, including a pineapple wine made from locally grown pineapples and reds and whites made from grapes grown on Haleakala's slopes.

MauiWine

Another notable winery on the island is MauiWine, formerly known as Tedeschi Winery. The winery makes a variety of wines, including rosé, Chenin Blanc, and Malbec. MauiWine also provides tours and tastings, where visitors can learn about the winemaking process and sample some of their wines.

Vineyards at Ulupalakua

The largest winery on Maui is Ulupalakua Vineyards, which is located on the southern slopes of Haleakala. The winery makes several wines, including Syrah, Viognier, and Rosé. Ulupalakua Vineyards also has a tasting room and a restaurant where visitors can dine while admiring the surrounding scenery.

Winery in Maui

Maui Winery in Kula is famous for its pineapple wine made from locally grown pineapples. Other wines produced by the winery include rosé, Chenin blanc, and gewürztraminer.

The top ten wines in Maui

From pineapple wines to traditional grape varietals, Maui produces a wide range of wines. The top ten Maui wines are as follows:

White Maui

A crisp and refreshing white wine made from a blend of white grape varieties grown on Haleakala's slopes.

Splash in Maui

On a hot day, this light and fruity pineapple wine are ideal for sipping.

Lokelani Rosé Sparkling

A lovely sparkling wine made from Pinot Noir grapes, with raspberry and strawberry notes.

Malbec Rose Ranch

A full-bodied red wine with blackberry and dark chocolate notes.

Maui Splash Red

A sweet red wine made from a grape and fruit juice blend, with black cherry and raspberry notes.

The Maui Rosé

Rosé made from Syrah grapes that are light and refreshing, with strawberry and watermelon flavors.

Pineapple, Passionfruit, and Maui Splash

A tropical twist on a classic pineapple wine, with the addition of passionfruit juice for a flavor burst.

Mango Splash Maui

A sweet and fruity pineapple wine with mango juice infusion.

Pineapple Splash from Maui

A traditional pineapple wine made from pineapples grown locally, with citrus and tropical fruit notes.

Syrah

A powerful and complex red wine with black cherry, black pepper, and tobacco flavors.

Restaurants on Maui that are highly recommended

Here are some restaurants that you should try during your visit:

Mama's Fish House

Mama's Fish House, located in Paia, is a must-see for seafood enthusiasts. The restaurant serves fresh fish caught daily by local fishermen, with dishes like the famous stuffed Mahi Mahi and grilled opah on the menu.

The Lahaina Grill

This Lahaina restaurant is well-known for its inventive and flavorful dishes. The macadamia nut-crusted goat cheese appetizer and the Kona coffee-rubbed lamb chops are among the dishes on the menu.

The Mill House

The Mill House, located in a beautiful tropical setting in Waikapu, serves farm-to-table cuisine made with fresh local ingredients. The roasted beet and goat cheese salad and the pork belly with pineapple chutney are two dishes on the menu.

Hali'imaile General Store

For over 30 years, this casual Hali'imaile restaurant has been a Maui favorite. Szechuan pork and macadamia nut-crusted chicken are among the dishes on the menu.

Gannon's

Gannon's, located in Wailea, offers stunning views of the ocean and a variety of delectable dishes, such as seared ahi and Maui onion soup.

Monkeypod Restaurant

This Wailea family-friendly restaurant is known for its inventive cocktails and delicious food. Wood-fired pizzas and seared scallops are on the menu.

Kula Bistro

This charming Kula bistro is a hidden treasure. Menu items include mushroom and truffle oil pizza and braised short ribs.

Leoda's Kitchen and Pie Shop

This popular Lahaina restaurant is known for its delicious homemade pies, but the menu also includes savory options like fish tacos and roast beef sandwiches.

Merriman's

Merriman's in Kapalua serves farm-to-table cuisine made with locally sourced ingredients. Seared scallops and grilled lamb chops are among the dishes on the menu.

Noodle of the Stars

This Lahaina noodle shop serves tasty dishes like garlic noodles and pork buns. There are also Asian-inspired small plates on the menu.

Whatever cuisine you crave, Maui has a restaurant to satisfy it. These recommended restaurants will impress your taste buds and provide an unforgettable dining experience, from fresh seafood to farm-to-table cuisine.

Chapter 5: Activities and entertainment

Sports

Here are some of the best sports to do in Maui:

Surfing

Maui is famous for its world-class waves, making it a popular destination for surfers of all abilities. From beginner-friendly spots like Lahaina and Kihei to more advanced spots like Honolua Bay and Peahi, the island has a variety of breaks (known as Jaws).

SUP (Stand-Up Paddleboarding)

SUP is a fun and easy way to explore Maui's calm bays and beaches. SUP is popular at Kaanapali and Makena Beaches.

Snorkeling

Maui offers some of the best snorkeling in Hawaii, thanks to its clear waters and vibrant coral reefs. Molokini Crater, Honolua Bay, and Ahihi-Kinau Natural Area Reserve are popular snorkeling destinations.

Scuba diving is a sport

Maui offers a variety of dive sites for more experienced divers, including lava tubes, caves, and shipwrecks. A wide variety of marine life, including sea turtles, rays, and sharks, can be found on the island.

Golf

The Plantation Course at Kapalua and the Wailea Golf Club are just two of Maui's world-class golf courses. The scenic courses on the island provide stunning views of the ocean and mountains.

Hiking

Maui has a wide range of hiking trails, from easy walks to strenuous treks. The Pipiwai Trail in Haleakala National Park and the Waihee Ridge Trail are popular hikes.

Tennis

Visitors can use the tennis courts at the Wailea Tennis Club and the Kapalua Tennis Garden on Maui.

Kitesurfing and windsurfing

Maui is a popular destination for windsurfing and kitesurfing because of its consistent trade winds. Kanaha Beach and Ho'okipa Beach Park are popular tourist destinations.

Sportfishing

Maui has excellent sportfishing opportunities, including marlin, tuna, and mahi-mahi. Charter fishing trips leave from Lahaina Harbor and Maalaea Harbor.

Yoga

Maui is an ideal place to practice yoga because of its beautiful natural surroundings and laid-back vibe. Yoga classes are available in many hotels and resorts, and there are several yoga studios located throughout the island.

Beaches

Maui is known for its beautiful beaches. Maui is a beach lover's dream, with its year-round sunny climate, crystal-clear waters, and soft white sand. Here are some of Maui's best beaches to visit:

The beach of Kaanapali

Kaanapali Beach is one of Maui's most popular beaches, located on the island's west coast. Its three miles of white sand and calm waters are ideal for swimming, snorkeling, and sunbathing.

The beach at Wailea

Wailea Beach is known for its soft golden sand and clear turquoise waters and is located in the upscale Wailea resort area. Swimming, snorkeling, and sunbathing are all popular activities on the beach.

Beach in Napili Bay

Napili Bay Beach, located in a secluded cove on Maui's northwest coast, is a hidden gem. Its sheltered waters and gentle surf make it ideal for families with children, and the scenic setting is ideal for a romantic sunset stroll.

Makena Beach

Makena Beach, also known as "Big Beach," is found on Maui's south shore. Its two-mile stretch of golden sand and turquoise waters is a popular swimming, boogie boarding, and sunbathing location.

The beach of Kapalua Bay

This beautiful crescent-shaped beach is on Maui's west coast. It is a popular snorkeling and swimming spot due to its calm waters and protected bay.

Park at Kamaole Beach

Kamaole Beach Park, located in Kihei, consists of three separate beaches, each with its distinct vibe. Swimming, snorkeling, and sunbathing are popular activities on the beaches.

The bay of Honolua

Honolua Bay, on Maui's northwest coast, is a popular snorkeling and diving location. A variety of colorful marine life, including sea turtles and tropical fish, lives in the bay's crystal-clear waters.

Kanaha Beach Park

Kanaha Beach Park is a popular spot for windsurfing, kitesurfing, and paddleboarding because of its strong winds and calm waters.

Swimming and sunbathing are also popular activities at the beach.

The beach at Hamoa

Hamoa Beach, located on Maui's east coast, is famous for its dramatic scenery and turquoise waters. The beach is surrounded by lush green cliffs and offers excellent swimming and bodyboarding opportunities.

Park at Ho'okipa Beach

Ho'okipa Beach Park, on Maui's north shore, is a popular spot for surfing, windsurfing, and kitesurfing. The beach is also an excellent location for observing sea turtles and humpback whales.

Hiking

Maui is well-known for its beautiful beaches and tropical climate, but it is also a hiker's dream. From easy coastal walks to challenging mountain treks, the island offers a variety of hiking trails to suit all levels of fitness and experience. The following are some of the best hiking trails on Maui:

National Park of Haleakala

The Haleakala volcano, Maui's highest peak, is located in Haleakala National Park. Hiking trails wind through volcanic landscapes, bamboo forests, and native Hawaiian plants at the park. The Sliding Sands Trail, which descends 2,800 feet into the volcano's crater, is a popular hike, while the Pipiwai Trail leads hikers through a lush bamboo forest to the beautiful Waimoku Falls.

The state park of Iao Valley

Iao Valley State Park in central Maui offers a variety of short hiking trails that showcase the park's stunning natural beauty. The Iao Needle, a 1,200-foot-tall rock formation, is the park's main attraction. Hiking trails in the park wind through tropical rainforests and along the Iao Stream's banks.

The Waihee Ridge Trail

The Waihee Ridge Trail is a difficult hike with spectacular views of Maui's north shore. The path winds through a lush forest of native Hawaiian plants such as koa and ohia trees before emerging onto a ridge with panoramic views of the ocean and surrounding valleys.

Pipiwai Track

The Pipiwai Trail leads hikers through a lush bamboo forest to the stunning Waimoku Falls in Haleakala National Park. With gentle inclines and well-maintained paths, the trail is suitable for hikers of all fitness levels.

Trail of the Lahaina Pali

The Lahaina Pali Trail is a historic hiking path that winds through the West Maui Mountains. Beautiful views of the ocean and the neighboring islands of Molokai and Lanai can be had from the trail. The trail is difficult, with steep inclines and rocky terrain, but the views are well worth the effort.

Coastal Path of Kapalua

The Kapalua Coastal Trail winds along Maui's west coast and is a pleasant, scenic hike. The trail provides breathtaking views of the ocean and the neighboring islands of Molokai and Lanai, as well as passing by several beautiful beaches.

The trail to the Twin Falls

The Twin Falls Trail is a short, easy hike that leads hikers through a lush tropical forest to two beautiful waterfalls. The trail is popular among families because it allows them to cool off in the cool waters of the falls.

Makawao Forest Reserve

Hiking trails wind through a forest of eucalyptus trees and native Hawaiian plants in the Makawao Forest Reserve. The Kahakapao Loop Trail is a well-known hike that provides breathtaking views of the surrounding mountains and valleys.

The Kealia Pond National Wildlife Refuge

The Kealia Pond National Wildlife Refuge is home to a variety of native Hawaiian birds and has several hiking trails that wind through wetlands and along the shoreline. The Kanaha Pond Trail is a flat, easy hike with spectacular views of the ocean and the neighboring island of Kahoolawe.

Polipoli Spring State Park

The Polipoli Spring State Recreation Area in upcountry Maui offers a variety of hiking trails that wind through a forest of towering trees and ferns. The Redwood Trail is a popular hiking trail that provides breathtaking views of the surrounding mountains and valleys.

Markets

Maui is a beautiful Hawaiian island with a variety of markets for visitors to explore. Maui's markets offer an excellent opportunity to experience the island's culture and lifestyle, with everything from fresh produce and handmade crafts to unique souvenirs and local specialties.

The Maui Swap Meet, which takes place every Saturday from 7 a.m. to 1 p.m. at the University of Hawaii Maui College in Kahului, is one of the most popular markets on Maui. This market sells a wide variety of goods, such as fresh produce, handmade crafts, clothing, jewelry, and other items. Souvenirs such as Hawaiian shirts, leis, and other traditional items are available to visitors. The Maui Swap Meet is a great place to experience local culture and find one-of-a-kind gifts to take home.

The Lahaina Farmers Market, which is located in the heart of Lahaina town, is another popular market in Maui. This market sells fresh produce, including locally grown fruits and vegetables, as well as handcrafted items, clothing, and jewelry. The Lahaina Farmers Market is open daily from 7 a.m. to 7 p.m., making it an ideal stop for visitors looking to immerse themselves in local culture while stocking up on fresh produce.

The Maui County Farm Bureau Farmers Market is a great option for those seeking a more traditional Hawaiian market experience. This market is held at the Maui Tropical Plantation in Waikapu on Tuesdays, Wednesdays, and Fridays from 7 a.m. to 11 a.m. Fresh produce, such as fruits and vegetables grown on the island, as well as locally made products such as honey, jams, and baked goods, are available to visitors.

The Maui Arts and Cultural Center (MACC) Craft Fair is worth visiting if you're looking for a market that offers a one-of-a-kind shopping experience. This market is held on the first Sunday of each month from 10 a.m. to 5 p.m. and features over 50 local artisans selling their handmade crafts such as jewelry, clothing, pottery, and other items. The

MACC Craft Fair is a fantastic place to find unique souvenirs and gifts.

Getting to the markets in Maui is simple, and there are several options for transportation. Many visitors to Maui choose to rent a car to explore the island at their leisure. Most markets provide free parking, allowing visitors to park their cars and browse the stalls for as long as they like.

There are several public transportation options available for those who prefer not to drive. The Maui Bus is an easy and inexpensive way to get around the island, and many of the markets are close to bus stops. Visitors can also take a taxi or Uber to the markets, though this will cost more than taking public transportation.

Finally, for visitors staying in Maui's resort areas, shuttle buses frequently run between hotels and popular attractions, including some markets. This can be a convenient option for those who don't want to deal with transportation and would rather someone else drive.

Shopping

Maui is a popular tourist destination for visitors from all over the world, and shopping is just one of the many activities available on the island.

The Whalers Village, located in the heart of Kaanapali, is one of Maui's most popular shopping destinations. This outdoor shopping center has a wide range of stores, including high-end luxury brands such as Louis Vuitton and Tiffany & Co. as well as more affordable options such as H&M and Sephora. Whalers Village has a variety of restaurants and entertainment options in addition to shopping, making it a great place to spend an afternoon or evening.

The Shops at Wailea, located in the upscale resort town of Wailea, is another popular shopping destination in Maui. Gucci, Prada, and Tiffany & Co. are among the luxury and designer brands represented at this shopping center. The Shops at Wailea provide a variety of dining and entertainment options, including a movie theater, in addition to shopping.

Maui offers a variety of markets and boutiques where visitors can find unique souvenirs and gifts. The Maui Swap Meet, held every Saturday at the University of Hawaii Maui College in Kahului, is one popular market. This market sells a wide range of items, including handcrafted items, clothing, and fresh produce. Visitors can also buy Hawaiian shirts and leis as souvenirs.

Lahaina is also a fantastic place to shop on Maui. It is a charming historic town with several shops, boutiques, and art galleries. Visitors can purchase one-of-a-kind souvenirs like Hawaiian-made crafts, jewelry, and clothing.

Getting to Maui's shopping destinations is simple, and there are several transportation options. Many visitors to Maui choose to rent a car to explore the island at their leisure. Most shopping malls and markets provide free parking, allowing visitors to leave their cars and spend as much time as they want shopping.

There are several public transportation options available for those who prefer not to drive. The Maui Bus is an easy and inexpensive way to get around the island, and many of the shopping areas are close to bus stops. Visitors can also take a taxi or Uber to the shopping malls, though this will be more expensive than taking public transportation.

Finally, for visitors staying in Maui's resort areas, shuttle buses frequently run between the hotels and popular shopping areas. This can be a convenient option for those who don't want to deal with transportation and would rather someone else drive.

Souvenirs

The Hawaiian shirt, also known as an aloha shirt, is one of the most popular souvenirs in Maui. These shirts, which are a staple of Hawaiian fashion, are frequently made with colorful, tropical patterns. Aloha shirts can be found in a variety of stores on Maui, ranging from souvenir shops to high-end boutiques. These shirts are ideal for wearing on the beach or a casual night out.

The lei, a traditional Hawaiian garland made of flowers, leaves, or shells, is another popular souvenir in Maui. Leis are a symbol of hospitality and are frequently used as a greeting or farewell gift. Leis can be purchased in a variety of stores throughout Maui and are ideal for wearing to a special event or as a decorative piece.

Maui has a variety of galleries and shops that feature the work of local artists for those who are interested in local art. Paintings, sculptures, and other works of art depict the island's natural beauty and distinctive culture. Many of these galleries also provide workshops and classes where visitors can learn more about the art and techniques used by local artists.

Handmade crafts are another popular Maui souvenir. Local artisans sell a variety of crafts, including wood carvings, woven baskets, and handmade jewelry. These crafts are frequently made from materials found on the island, such as koa wood and sea shells, and are ideal for incorporating a touch of Maui into your home decor.

Food items are also popular Maui souvenirs. Coffee, chocolate, and macadamia nuts are among the locally produced foods available to visitors. These items make wonderful gifts for foodies and can be enjoyed long after your Maui vacation is over.

Finally, for those interested in the island's history and culture, Maui sells hula skirts, ukuleles, and poi pounders. These items are ideal for learning more about the island's rich cultural heritage and making excellent souvenirs for those with an interest in Hawaiian history and traditions.

Nightlife

Watching the sunset is one of the most popular nightlife activities in Maui. The island has some of the most stunning sunsets in the world, and there are numerous vantage points from which to enjoy them. At the top of Haleakala, the island's tallest peak, one of the best places to watch the sunset. You can see the sun setting over the Pacific Ocean from here.

Dining out is another popular nightlife activity in Maui. On the island, numerous excellent restaurants are serving a wide range of cuisines, from traditional Hawaiian to international fare.

Lahaina, a historic town with many great restaurants and bars, is one of the best places to dine in Maui. Lahaina Grill, Merriman's, and Fleetwood's on Front St. are among the most popular restaurants in town.

Many people head to Maui's bars and nightclubs after dinner for a night of dancing and fun. The Dirty Monkey in Lahaina is one of the island's most popular nightclubs. The club has a lively vibe and frequently hosts live music performances by local bands and DJs. Lulu's Lahaina Surf Club & Grill, which has a more relaxed atmosphere and is known for its excellent drinks and food, is another popular nightclub.

Maui also has many bars and lounges where you can relax and enjoy a few drinks with friends for those who prefer a more low-key nightlife experience. Charley's Restaurant and Saloon, in Paia, is one of the best bars on the island. The bar has a cozy vibe and frequently hosts live music performances by local musicians. Fleetwood's on Front St. is another popular bar with a rooftop bar that overlooks the ocean.

Maui also hosts numerous cultural events at night. The Maui Arts and Cultural Center, which hosts a variety of events throughout the year, is one of the most well-known. The center is in Kahului and is a great place to learn about the culture and art scene on the island.

Maui offers several options for those interested in experiencing a traditional Hawaiian luau. The Old Lahaina Luau, which takes place in Lahaina and includes a delicious buffet dinner and a lively performance of traditional Hawaiian dance and music, is one of the most popular.

Finally, no discussion of Maui's nightlife is complete without mentioning the island's numerous beach parties. Many of the island's beaches host public parties and events during the summer months. The Friday night beach party at Little Beach in Makena is one of the most popular. The party has a laid-back vibe and frequently features live music and fire dancers.

Natural attractions

The natural beauty of the island stems from its distinct geography, which includes towering mountains, lush valleys, and a breathtaking coastline.

Haleakala National Park is a popular natural attraction in Maui. The park is home to the dormant Haleakala volcano, which at over 10,000 feet is the highest point on the island. Hiking to the summit provides visitors with spectacular views of the surrounding landscape, which includes lava fields, cinder cones, and rare plant and animal species. At sunrise, visitors gather to watch the sun rise above the clouds on Haleakala.

The Road to Hana is another natural wonder that draws visitors to Maui. This scenic drive follows the coast, providing breathtaking views of waterfalls, lush rainforests, and panoramic ocean vistas. Visitors can stop in charming small towns and hike to secluded beaches and hidden coves along the way. The road to Hana is popular for a day trip, but many visitors prefer to stay overnight in one of the area's charming bed and breakfasts to fully explore the region.

Maui's beaches are also popular with tourists. Maui's coastline has something for everyone, from the golden sands of Kaanapali Beach to the windsurfing paradise of Hookipa Beach. Wailea Beach, one of the most popular beaches on the island, has crystal-clear waters and excellent snorkeling opportunities. Hike to the remote and beautiful Kaihalulu Beach, also known as the Red

Sand Beach, for a more secluded beach experience, where the sand is a deep red color due to the iron-rich volcanic rocks in the area.

Maui also has several breathtaking waterfalls that are a must-see for nature lovers. The 400-foot Wailua Falls, one of the most famous waterfalls on the island, can be seen from a lookout point or by hiking down to the base of the falls. Twin Falls is another popular waterfall that is easily accessible and surrounded by lush vegetation and bamboo groves.

Maui is known for its distinct culture and history, in addition to its natural attractions. The Maui County Fair and the Maui Onion Festival, which showcase traditional Hawaiian music, dance, and cuisine, commemorate the island's rich cultural heritage. The Bailey House Museum, which features exhibits on the island's early settlers, the whaling industry, and sugar plantations, is also a great place to learn about Maui's history.

Finally, there are many activities available for those seeking a more adventurous way to experience Maui's natural attractions, such as hiking, snorkeling, and surfing. The rugged terrain of the island provides numerous hiking trails ranging from easy walks to challenging hikes for hikers of all skill levels. Water sports enthusiasts will enjoy snorkeling and diving in Maui's warm waters, where they can see a variety of marine life, including sea turtles, colorful fish, and even dolphins and whales. Surfing is another popular activity on the island, which has several world-renowned surf spots, including Honolua Bay and Pe'ahi, also known as Jaws, which has some of the world's largest waves.

Maui's festivals

The Maui County Fair, which takes place every September, is one of the most popular festivals on the island. The fair honors Maui's rich agricultural heritage with livestock shows, exhibitions, and competitions. Visitors can enjoy carnival rides, live music, and a wide selection of delectable local cuisine. The fair is a great place to learn about local culture and meet Maui residents.

The Maui Onion Festival, held in May, is another popular Maui event. The festival honors the Maui Onion, a rare and delicious variety of onion grown only on Maui. Visitors can sample a variety of Maui Onion-inspired dishes such as onion rings, onion soup, and onion burgers. Live music, arts and crafts, and a farmers' market are also part of the festival.

The Maui Film Festival, which takes place in June, is another popular festival in Maui. The festival honors the art of filmmaking by screening independent films from all over the world. Panel discussions with filmmakers and actors, as well as outdoor screenings under the stars, are also part of the festival. Visitors can enjoy the stunning Maui scenery while watching some of the world's best films.

The Maui Jazz and Blues Festival, which takes place in September, is a celebration of jazz and blues music. Some of the world's top jazz and blues musicians, as well as local talent, will perform at the festival. Visitors can listen to live music while admiring the stunning scenery of Maui.

In May, the Maui Matsuri festival celebrates Japanese culture. Traditional Japanese music, dance, and food, as well as arts and crafts, are all featured at the festival. Tea ceremonies, martial arts demonstrations, and traditional Japanese crafts are all available to visitors.

Another popular July festival in Maui is the Makawao Rodeo. The festival honors the island's cowboy culture with rodeo events such as bull riding, barrel racing, and team roping. Live music, food vendors, and a parade are also available to visitors.

The Maui Whale Festival commemorates the annual migration of humpback whales to Maui. From December to May, the festival offers a variety of events such as whale-watching tours, educational lectures, and live music. Visitors can learn about whales and their migration patterns while also admiring Maui's stunning coastline.

The Lahaina Halloween Festival is a family-friendly Halloween celebration held in October. A costume contest, live music, and a variety of activities for children are all part of the festival. Visitors can get into the Halloween spirit while enjoying Maui's beautiful weather.

Chapter 6: Itenararies

What to do in 48 hours in Maui

Here are some suggestions for what to do in Maui in 48 hours:

Day 1:

- Begin your day with a sunrise viewing at Haleakala National Park. As the sun rises above the clouds from the summit of a volcano, you will have an unforgettable experience.

- Hike one of the park's numerous trails after sunrise. Both the Pipiwai and Sliding Sands trails are excellent choices.

- Drive the scenic Road to Hana, which winds through lush rainforests, waterfalls, and small towns. Along the way, visit the Garden of Eden Arboretum, Keanae Peninsula, and Wailua Falls.

- End your day at the beach by watching the sunset. Maui's best sunset-viewing beaches include Kaanapali Beach and Napili Bay.

Day 2:

- Visit Molokini, a crescent-shaped volcanic crater with incredible underwater visibility and diverse marine life.

- Visit Lahaina, a historically preserved whaling town. Visit Lahaina Harbor and the Baldwin Home Museum while strolling down Front Street, which is lined with galleries, shops, and restaurants.

- Take a picnic lunch at the Maui Ocean Center, which is home to a variety of marine life and has breathtaking views of the ocean.

- Finish the day with a sunset dinner cruise, where you can eat a delicious meal while watching the sunset over the ocean.

- Of course, there are many other activities on Maui, such as surfing, hiking, and visiting the Maui Tropical Plantation, among others. However, in just 48 hours, these activities will give you a taste of the island's natural beauty and culture.

What to do in Maui in a week

Maui is a lovely Hawaiian island with plenty to do and see during a seven-day visit. Here are some itinerary suggestions to get you started:

Day 1:

- Begin your trip with a day at the beach. Maui's top beaches include Kaanapali Beach, Kapalua Beach, and Makena Beach.
- In the evening, stroll down Lahaina's Front Street and check out the shops and restaurants.

Day 2:

- Travel to Molokini Crater for snorkeling or diving. This crescent-shaped volcanic crater is home to some of Maui's best snorkeling and diving.
- Spend the remainder of the day exploring Kihei, a charming town with many restaurants and shops.

Day 3:

- Drive the Road to Hana and stop at the many scenic spots along the way, including the Garden of Eden Arboretum, the Keanae Peninsula, and Wailua Falls.
- Spend the night in Hana and soak up the laid-back atmosphere.

Day 4:

- Visit Haleakala National Park and witness the sunrise from the volcano's summit.
- Take a hike in the park and take in the breathtaking scenery.

Day 5:

- Take a day trip to Lanai, a neighboring island that is more secluded and peaceful than Maui.
- Explore the beautiful beaches and hiking trails on the island.

Day 6:

- Take a whale-watching tour (during the season) to get up close and personal with these magnificent creatures.
- The Maui Ocean Center, which features a variety of marine life and interactive exhibits, is worth a visit.

Day 7:

- Take a helicopter tour of Maui to see the island from a different angle.
- Unwind at a spa with a massage or other treatment.
- Of course, there are numerous other activities on Maui, such as surfing and visiting the Iao Valley State Park. However, this itinerary should give you a good idea of what the island has to offer throughout a seven-day trip.

Chapter 7: Accommodation and transportation in Maui

Accommodation and transportation are two critical factors to consider when planning a trip to Maui. We'll go over some of the best options for both in this guide, so you can make the most of your time on the island.

Maui lodging

Maui offers a diverse selection of lodging options, including hotels, resorts, vacation rentals, and bed and breakfasts. Here are some of the most popular options:

Resorts and hotels

There are numerous luxury hotels and resorts in Maui that provide world-class amenities and services. These properties are ideal for vacationers looking for a luxurious experience. The Four Seasons Resort Maui at Wailea, Grand Wailea, and Fairmont Kea Lani are among the most popular resorts.

Vacation rentals

For families and groups of friends traveling together, vacation rentals are an excellent choice. Maui has a wide range of vacation rental properties to choose from, including cozy beach cottages and luxurious villas. Websites such as Airbnb and VRBO provide a diverse selection of vacation rentals.

Bed and breakfast

For those seeking a more personalized experience, bed and Breakfast is an excellent choice. Maui has a plethora of charming bed and breakfasts that provide comfortable lodging and delectable breakfasts. The Old Wailuku Inn at Ulupono, the Ho'oilo House, and the Maui Seaside Hotel are among the top options.

Top hotels in Maui

This guide will discuss the top ten best hotels in Maui, as well as how to get there.

Wailea Four Seasons Resort

The Four Seasons Resort Maui at Wailea is a luxurious resort on the island of Maui's southwest coast. It has large rooms, five pools, and a variety of dining options. To get there, fly into Kahului Airport and then drive south for about 35 minutes to Wailea.

Kapalua Bay Montage

The Montage Kapalua Bay is a luxury resort on Maui's north west coast. It has breathtaking views of the ocean, spacious suites, and an on-site spa. Fly to Kapalua Airport, which is only a few minutes away from the resort.

Wailea Resort

The Hotel Wailea is an adults-only resort on the island of Maui's southwest coast. It has luxurious suites, an infinity pool, and several dining options. To get there, fly into Kahului Airport and then drive south for about 30 minutes to Wailea.

The Andaz Maui Resort at Wailea

The Andaz Maui at Wailea Resort is a luxurious resort on the island of Maui's southwest coast. It has large rooms, several pools, and a variety of dining options. To get there, fly into Kahului Airport and then drive south for about 35 minutes to Wailea.

Fairmont Kea Lani Hotel

The Fairmont Kea Lani is a luxurious resort on the island of Maui's southwest coast. It has large suites, several pools, and a variety of dining options. To get there, fly into Kahului Airport and then drive south for about 30 minutes to Wailea.

Travaasa Hana

The Travaasa Hana, Maui is a luxurious resort on the island's eastern coast. It has large rooms, a variety of activities, and a spa on-site. To get there, fly to Kahului Airport and then drive the Hana Highway for about 2 hours.

Kapalua Ritz-Carlton

The Ritz-Carlton Kapalua is a luxury resort on Maui's north west coast. It has large rooms, several pools, and a variety of dining options. Fly to Kapalua Airport, which is only a few minutes away from the resort.

Wailea Grand

The Grand Wailea is a luxurious resort on the island of Maui's southwest coast. It has large rooms, several pools, and a variety of dining options. To get there, fly into Kahului Airport and then drive south for about 35 minutes to Wailea.

Hyatt Regency Maui Resort and Spa

The Hyatt Regency Maui Resort and Spa is a luxurious resort on the island of Maui's west coast. It has large rooms, several pools, and a variety of dining options. To get there, fly to Kahului Airport and then drive west for 45 minutes to Kaanapali.

The Westin Maui Resort and Spa

The Westin Maui Resort and Spa is a luxurious resort on the island of Maui's western coast. It has large rooms, several pools, and a variety of dining options. To get there, fly to Kahului Airport and then drive west for 45 minutes to Kaanapali.

Convenient mode of transportation in Maui

Vehicle Rental

One of the most convenient ways to get around Maui is to rent a car. You can rent a car at the Kahului Airport or several other locations on the island. Maui's road system is well-maintained, and driving allows you to explore the island at your leisure. You can visit the island's various beaches, drive along the scenic Road to Hana, and explore the small towns and villages. Renting a car also allows you to plan your itinerary and visit the attractions that are most interesting to you. However, during peak tourist season, traffic can be congested and parking can be difficult in some areas.

Public transportation

The Maui Bus operates a public transportation system on Maui. The bus system covers the majority of the island, and fares are reasonable. It is an excellent choice for budget-conscious travelers who want to explore the island without having to pay for a car rental. The buses run seven days a week, and schedules can be found online. It is important to note, however, that the bus service can be slow and infrequent, and it is not always convenient for exploring remote areas.

Taxi

Taxis are widely available on Maui and are an excellent choice for short trips or when you don't want to drive. They are especially helpful in getting around larger towns and cities like Lahaina, Kihei, and Kahului. Taxis are metered, and fares can be high, especially for longer trips. It is also important to keep in mind that taxis may not be readily available in remote areas of the island, and you may need to make a reservation in advance.

Uber and Lyft

Uber and Lyft are both available on Maui, and they provide a convenient and cost-effective way to get around the island. Ride-sharing services are especially convenient for short trips or when you do not want to drive. They're also a great way to check out the nightlife in larger towns and cities. Uber and Lyft fares are typically less expensive than taxi fares, and they provide a more convenient and dependable mode of transportation. It is important to note, however, that ride-sharing services may be unavailable in remote areas of the island, and wait times may be longer during peak tourist season.

Bicycle

Biking is an excellent way to explore Maui, especially for environmentally conscious visitors.

On the island, there are several bike rental shops where you can rent a bike for the day or longer. Biking allows you to explore the island at your own pace and gain access to some of the more remote areas not accessible by car. Cycling is another great way to stay active while taking in scenic views of the island. It is important to note, however, that biking can be difficult in some areas of the island, particularly on hilly terrain. It is also critical to wear proper safety equipment, such as helmets and reflective clothing, and to be aware of oncoming traffic.

How to use the Maui transportation system

Getting around Maui can be difficult, especially if you are unfamiliar with the island's road system and public transportation system. In this guide, we'll go over some transportation tips for Maui to help you get the most out of your trip.

Make a plan for your trip

It is critical to plan your itinerary and decide which attractions to visit before arriving in Maui. This will assist you in determining which mode of transportation is best for each activity. Renting a car, for example, maybe the most convenient option if you plan to explore the Road to Hana. If you want to visit larger towns and cities, such as Lahaina and Kihei, taking public transportation, taxis, or using ride-sharing services may be more convenient.

Rent a vehicle

One of the most convenient ways to get around Maui is to rent a car. It allows you to explore the island at your own pace and see the attractions that most interest you. It is critical to book a car rental in advance, especially during peak tourist season. It is also critical to carefully read the rental agreement and understand the terms and conditions, which include insurance coverage, fuel policy, and mileage restrictions.

Make use of the Maui Bus

The Maui Bus is the island's public transportation system and an inexpensive way to get around. The buses run seven days a week, and schedules can be found online. When taking the Maui Bus, it is critical to plan your route ahead of time and carefully check the schedules. Some routes may be infrequent, especially on weekends and holidays, so plan ahead of time.

Consider taking a taxi or using a ride-sharing service

On Maui, taxis and ride-sharing services like Uber and Lyft are readily available. They're ideal for short trips or when you don't want to drive. Taxis are metered, and fares can be high, especially for longer trips. Taxis are generally more expensive than ride-sharing services, but they may not be available in all areas of the island. When taking a taxi or using a ride-sharing service, it is critical to book ahead of time, especially during peak tourist season.

Hire a bike

Biking is a popular way to explore Maui, especially among eco-conscious visitors. On the island, there are several bike rental shops where you can rent a bike for the day or longer. Biking allows you to explore the island at your own pace and gain access to some of the more remote areas not accessible by car. However, it is critical to be aware of on-road traffic and to wear appropriate safety equipment, such as helmets and reflective clothing.

Keep an eye on the traffic

During the peak tourist season, traffic on Maui can become congested, particularly in the larger towns and cities. It's critical to pay attention to traffic and plan your routes accordingly. It is critical to follow speed limits and be aware of other drivers on the road when driving. When taking public transportation, it is critical to account for traffic delays and schedule changes.

Utilize GPS

When navigating transportation in Maui, using GPS can be beneficial, especially if you are unfamiliar with the island's road network. GPS is standard in most rental cars, but you can also use your smartphone or a standalone GPS device. When using GPS, keep the maps up to date and be aware of any road closures or detours.

Chapter 8: Packing list

If you're heading to Maui, here's a packing list to make sure you've got everything you need:

Swimwear: Because Maui is known for its beautiful beaches and crystal clear waters, bring your swimsuits or board shorts with you.

Sunscreen: Because the sun is so strong in Maui, you should bring sunscreen to protect your skin. Choose a sunscreen with an SPF of 30 or higher.

Sunglasses: To protect your eyes from the harsh sunlight, bring a pair of sunglasses with you.

Clothes: Because Maui is hot and humid, pack lightweight clothing made of breathable fabrics like cotton or linen.

Hiking shoes or sandals: Bring a pair of comfortable shoes or sandals that can handle rough terrain if you intend to hike or explore.

Water bottle: Because staying hydrated is critical in Maui's hot climate, bring a reusable water bottle to refill throughout the day.

Snorkeling equipment: Because Maui is known for its beautiful coral reefs and marine life, bring your snorkeling equipment if you intend to explore the underwater world.

Insect repellent: Because mosquitoes can be a problem in some areas of Maui, bring insect repellent with you to avoid bites.

Camera: Bring a camera or phone to capture your memories of Maui's stunning landscapes.

Cash: While most places in Maui accept credit cards, having some cash on hand for smaller purchases or tips is always a good idea.

Hat: Pack a hat to keep the sun off your face and scalp. A wide-brimmed hat is ideal for providing full sun protection.

Light jacket: Even though Maui is warm, temperatures can drop in the evenings, particularly at higher elevations. To stay warm, bring a light jacket or sweater.

Beach towel: Pack a beach towel for lounging on the sand.

Toiletries: Bring your toothbrush, toothpaste, shampoo, conditioner, soap, and any other personal care items with you.

Medications: Bring any prescription or over-the-counter medications you may require during your trip.

Adapter: Bring a travel adapter if you're traveling from another country.

Documents: Bring your passport or identification, airline tickets, hotel reservations, and any other important travel documents.

Portable charger: Carry a portable charger with you to keep your phone or camera charged while you're on the go.

Books or e-reader: Unwind on the beach with a good book, or bring your e-reader for quick access to your favorite books.

Snacks: Bring some snacks with you to munch on while traveling, such as energy bars, trail mix, or fruit. This is useful for long hikes or trips to the beach.

First Aid Kit: small first aid kit containing bandages, antiseptic wipes, pain relievers, and other basic medical supplies is always a good idea.

Bags: Bring ziplock bags to store wet swimsuits, dirty clothes, or any other items that might leak.

Pillow: A travel pillow can help make a long flight or car ride more comfortable.

Detergent: If you intend to do laundry during your trip, bring some travel-size laundry detergent with you.

Reusable bags: Bring reusable bags with you for grocery shopping or carrying souvenirs.

Waterproof phone case: If you're going to the beach or pool, bring a waterproof phone case to protect your phone from water damage.

Binoculars: Bring a pair of binoculars if you intend to do some whale or bird watching.

Blanket: A cashmere or lightweight blanket can help make a long flight more comfortable.

Water shoes: Bring a pair of water shoes if you plan on doing water sports or walking on rocky beaches.

Packing list for females

If you're a female traveler heading to Maui, here's a packing list to make sure you've got everything you need:

Sun hat: Pack a sun hat to protect your face and scalp from the sun. A wide-brimmed hat is ideal for providing full sun protection.

Swimsuits: Because Maui is known for its beautiful beaches and crystal clear waters, bring your swimsuits with you.

Sunscreen: Because the sun is so strong in Maui, you should bring sunscreen to protect your skin. Choose a sunscreen with an SPF of 30 or higher.

Sunglasses: To protect your eyes from the harsh sunlight, bring a pair of sunglasses with you.

Clothes: Because Maui is hot and humid, pack lightweight clothing made of breathable fabrics like cotton or linen.

Hiking shoes or sandals: Bring a pair of comfortable shoes or sandals that can handle rough terrain if you intend to hike or explore.

Water bottle: Because staying hydrated is critical in Maui's hot climate, bring a reusable water bottle to refill throughout the day.

Snorkeling equipment: Because Maui is known for its beautiful coral reefs and marine life, bring your snorkeling equipment if you intend to explore the underwater world.

Insect repellent: Because mosquitoes can be a problem in some areas of Maui, bring insect repellent with you to avoid bites.

Bring a camera or phone: to capture your memories of Maui's stunning landscapes.

Pack a lightweight **cardigan** or shawl for evenings or cool days.

Pack a pair of **sandals or flip-flops** to wear around the resort or on the beach.

A **maxi dress** is a versatile item that can be dressed up or down, making it ideal for exploring the island or going out to dinner.

Moisturizer: The climate on Maui can be dry, so bring some to keep your skin hydrated.

Bring some **makeup wipes** with you for easy makeup removal.

A **bathing suit** cover-up is a great item to have on hand for beach days or poolside lounging.

Pack travel-size **shampoo, conditioner**, and other **hair care products** to save space in your suitcase.

Remember to bring any **feminine hygiene products** you may require during your trip.

Bring travel-sized **skincare products such as cleansers, toners, and moisturizers** with you to keep your skin looking its best.

Bring some **plastic bags** with you to store wet swimsuits or dirty clothes.

Even though Maui is warm, temperatures can drop in the evenings, especially at higher elevations. To stay warm, bring a **light jacket or sweater**.

Pack enough **bras, underwear, and socks** for your trip.

Bring some travel-sized **laundry detergent** if you plan on doing laundry while on vacation.

Bring reusable bags with you for grocery shopping or carrying souvenirs.

Portable charger: Carry a portable charger with you to keep your phone or camera charged while you're on the go.

Maui money-saving ideas

Maui can be an expensive destination. The costs of flights and accommodations, as well as activities and dining, can quickly add up. There are, however, ways to save money on your Maui vacation without sacrificing enjoyment. Here are some money-saving suggestions to help you get the most out of your trip.

Off-season travel

Traveling to Maui during the off-season is one of the simplest ways to save money on your vacation. Typically, the off-season runs from April to May and September to November. You can find a cheaper airfare, hotel rates, and tour prices during this time. You'll also avoid crowds and enjoy a more relaxing vacation.

Plan ahead of time

Another way to save money is to plan ahead of time. This includes airfare, lodging, and activities. Many airlines and hotels provide early booking discounts, so look for them. You can also avoid peak season rates and ensure availability for popular activities and attractions by booking ahead of time.

Consider other options

While there are many luxury resorts in Maui, there are also less expensive options. Consider renting a vacation home, staying in a hostel, or going camping. Vacation rental sites such as Airbnb and VRBO provide a wide range of options, from low-cost studios to large homes that can accommodate large groups. Hostels offer shared lodging for backpackers and other low-cost travelers. Camping is an additional option, with several campgrounds on the island offering basic amenities and breathtaking views.

Take advantage of public transportation

Renting a car may appear to be the most convenient option, but it is also the most expensive. Maui has a well-developed public transportation system, including buses and shuttles. The Maui Bus serves the entire island, with fares starting at $2 per ride. Airport transfers and transportation to popular attractions and activities are provided by shuttles such as SpeediShuttle and Maui Airport Shuttle.

Utilize free activities

Hiking and beachcombing are two of the many free activities available on Maui. Hiking to the summit of Haleakala for sunrise or sunset, visiting the Maui Ocean Center on the first Sunday of the month for free admission, and exploring the island's many beautiful beaches are all popular activities. Throughout the year, the island also hosts several free events, such as festivals and concerts.

Bring your snacks and beverages

While there are many excellent restaurants and bars in Maui, dining out can be costly. Consider bringing your food and beverages to save money. Pack a cooler with snacks and beverages for the day, and prepare meals in your lodging. Costco, Walmart, and Safeway are just a few of the grocery stores in Maui.

Make use of coupon websites

Many discount websites provide discounts on activities, dining, and lodging. Discounts on tours, spa treatments, and restaurant meals can be found on websites such as Groupon and LivingSocial. Hotels.com and Expedia both provide discounted lodging rates. Check these sites before making any reservations to see if you can save money.

Look for places that offer free Wi-Fi

Look for free Wi-Fi if you need to stay connected during your trip. Customers can access free Wi-Fi at many hotels, restaurants, and coffee shops. Maui also has several public Wi-Fi access points, such as libraries and parks.

Take advantage of loyalty programs

If you travel frequently, consider joining airline, hotel, and car rental loyalty programs. These programs provide benefits such as complimentary upgrades, early check-in, and exclusive discounts. You can save money on future trips by accruing points or miles.

Shop at neighborhood markets

Maui has several farmers' markets and craft fairs where you can find one-of-a-kind souvenirs and gifts at a lower price than you would find in tourist shops. These markets also sell fresh produce, baked goods, and other locally produced goods at affordable prices. The Maui Swap Meet, Upcountry Farmers Market, and Lahaina Farmers Market are all popular markets.

Keep away from tourist traps

While it is tempting to visit popular tourist attractions, they are often expensive. Consider visiting less visited areas of Maui to save money. Explore the area's beaches, parks, and hiking trails. You might be surprised at what you discover if you venture off the beaten path.

Please bring your equipment

Consider bringing your snorkeling, kayaking, or surfing equipment if you plan on participating in activities such as these. Renting equipment can quickly add up, so bringing your own can save you money in the long run. You can also ensure a better fit and higher quality equipment by bringing your equipment.

Look for special offers

Many tour operators provide package deals that include multiple activities at a reduced cost. A package deal, for example, might include a snorkeling excursion, a luau, and a helicopter tour.

Before booking a package deal, compare prices and read reviews to ensure you're getting good value.

Make the most of happy hour

Many restaurants and bars have happy hour specials that include discounted food and drinks. Before dining out, make sure to check for happy hour times and specials. Furthermore, some restaurants provide early bird specials or prix fixe menus, which can help you save money.

Avoid wasting money

Finally, avoid unnecessary expenses to save money on your Maui vacation. ATM fees, resort fees, and credit card transaction fees are all examples of this. Before your trip, make sure to research these fees and plan accordingly.

Maui time-saving advice

Maui is a popular vacation destination with many activities to choose from, and it's easy to feel as if you don't have enough time to do it all. There are, however, some time-saving tips that can help you make the most of your trip and see everything Maui has to offer.

Plan your route ahead of time

Make a list of the activities and attractions you want to see before you go. Arrange them by location and date. This will allow you to make the most of your time on the island and avoid missing out on anything important.

Use early mornings to your advantage

Sunrises on Maui are known to be spectacular, so get up early to catch one. Furthermore, many popular attractions are less crowded in the early morning, allowing you to avoid the crowds and enjoy a more peaceful experience. Use the cooler morning temperatures to get a jump on your day.

Rent a vehicle

Renting a car allows you to explore the island at your own pace, saving you time. Maui's public transportation is limited, and taxis can be pricey. You can visit multiple attractions in one day by renting a car and avoiding the hassle of waiting for a bus or taxi.

Make use of GPS and mapping applications

With many winding paths and unfamiliar street names, Maui's roads can be perplexing. Using GPS and mapping apps can save you time by preventing you from getting lost or taking the wrong turn. If you don't have cellular service while exploring the island, be sure to download offline maps.

Make reservations for skip-the-line tours

Skip-the-line tours are available at many popular Maui attractions, allowing you to avoid long lines and save time. The Road to Hana, for example, is a popular attraction with numerous stops along the way; however, traffic can be slow and lines can be long. Booking a skip-the-line tour will allow you to avoid crowds and maximize your time on the road.

Think about private tours

Consider booking a private tour if you have specific activities or attractions you want to see. This is more expensive than a group tour, but it saves time by allowing you to customize your itinerary and avoid waiting for others in the group.

Pack lunch for a picnic

Dining out on Maui can take a long time, especially during peak hours. Pack a picnic lunch to save time and enjoy a meal in a scenic setting. There are many beautiful places on the island for a picnic lunch, such as the beach or a park.

Schedule activities ahead of time

Booking activities ahead of time can save you time by eliminating the need to wait in line or search for availability on the day of the activity. Many popular activities, such as snorkeling or zip lining, necessitate reservations. You can save time and have a more seamless experience if you book in advance.

Keep close to your activities

Choosing accommodations that are close to the activities you want to do can help you save time by reducing travel time. Consider staying in Hana or nearby if you want to explore the Road to Hana rather than in a more central location on the island.

Invest in travel apps

There are numerous travel apps available to help you save time on your Maui vacation. The Maui Bus app, for example, can assist you in planning your bus route and providing real-time updates on bus schedules. The Maui Beach app can assist you in finding nearby beaches as well as providing information on beach conditions and amenities.

Maui stress-reduction strategies

Although Maui is a beautiful and serene destination, travel can be stressful at times. There are ways to reduce stress and make the most of your Maui vacation, whether you're dealing with jet lag, trying to navigate a new place, or simply dealing with the usual travel stress.

Pack smartly

Packing wisely can help you stay stress-free during your trip. Bring comfortable shoes, sunscreen, and any medications that may be required. Plan your activities ahead of time and bring appropriate clothing and equipment. You can avoid the stress of feeling ill-prepared or uncomfortable by packing strategically.

Allow yourself some time to unwind

Maui is a place to unwind and rejuvenate. Allow yourself to unwind by the pool, on the beach, or at a spa. To reduce stress and find inner peace, try yoga or meditation. Maui is also known for its natural beauty, so take a moment to appreciate your surroundings and soak in the natural peace.

Get enough rest

Getting enough sleep is essential for reducing stress. Jet lag can be a major source of stress, so try to adjust your sleep schedule as much as possible before your trip. To help you adjust to the new time zone, try to keep a consistent sleep schedule once you arrive.

Overscheduling should be avoided

It may be tempting to try to pack as many activities as possible into your trip, but doing so can lead to stress and exhaustion. Make time for relaxation and unplanned activities. Keep in mind that quality over quantity is important, and it is preferable to fully enjoy a few activities rather than rush through many.

Consume healthily

Eating nutritious, healthy foods can help reduce stress and improve overall health. Take advantage of the many healthy dining options on the island, as Maui is known for its fresh, locally sourced foods. In the tropical climate, drinking plenty of water can also help reduce stress and keep you hydrated.

Self-care is important

Self-care is an essential component of stress reduction. Spend time doing something you enjoy, such as reading a book, going for a walk, or napping. To help you relax and rejuvenate, consider scheduling a massage or other spa treatment.

Make good use of technology

While technology can be beneficial when traveling, it can also be stressful. Try to use technology with caution and avoid using your phone or other devices excessively. To reduce the temptation to constantly check your phone, set aside specific times for checking emails or social media.

Maintain your organizational skills

Staying organized during your trip can help reduce stress. Important documents, such as passports and travel insurance, should be kept in a secure location. To reduce clutter and create a calming environment, keep your accommodations neat and organized. Use a travel app to help you keep track of reservations, activities, and other important information.

Practice being grateful

Gratitude exercises can help reduce stress and improve overall well-being. Take time to appreciate Maui's beauty and wonder, and be grateful for the experiences you're having. This can assist you in shifting your focus from stress to positivity and gratitude.

Be open-minded

Finally, it is critical to be adaptable and flexible during your journey. Unexpected events, such as flight delays or bad weather, can occur, so it's critical to maintain a flexible mindset and be willing to change your plans if necessary. Remember that your trip's goal is to relax and enjoy the beauty of Maui, which can be accomplished in a variety of ways.

Maui tourist do's and don'ts

The following are some of the most important tourist dos and don'ts in Maui:

Do's:

- **Take care of the environment**

Maui is a natural wonderland, and it's critical to respect the environment by adhering to the Leave No Trace principles. This includes not littering, adhering to designated trails, and not disturbing wildlife.

- **Dress properly**

While Maui is a relaxed destination, it is necessary to dress appropriately for various activities and occasions. For outdoor activities, bring appropriate clothing and footwear, and dress respectfully when visiting religious sites or attending cultural events.

- **Keep in mind the customs and culture of the area**

Visitors should be respectful of Maui's rich cultural history and traditions. Before your trip, research local customs and culture, and be mindful of your behavior and interactions with locals. When entering a house or temple, for example, it is customary to remove your shoes.

- **Help out your local businesses**

Local business support is an excellent way to contribute to the local economy and community. Consider purchasing locally made products as souvenirs from locally owned restaurants, shops, and tour companies.

- **Drive carefully**

Maui has many scenic drives, but driving responsibly is critical to your safety and the safety of others on the road. Maintain speed limits, drive defensively, and be aware of the island's unique driving conditions.

Don'ts:

- **Don't strew litter**

Littering is not only harmful to the environment, but it is also illegal on the island of Maui. To help preserve the natural beauty of the island, pack out all trash and dispose of it properly.

- **Do not offend religious sites**

Visitors should respect Maui's religious sites. When visiting these sites, avoid taking photos or disturbing worshipers, and dress appropriately.

- **Never approach or feed wildlife**

Maui is home to a variety of unique and beautiful wildlife species, but it is critical to respect their habitat and avoid disturbing them. Avoid touching or feeding wildlife and keep a safe distance from them.

- **Don't offend the locals**

Maui has a strong sense of community, so it's critical to respect the locals and their customs. Be mindful of your behavior and interactions with locals, and avoid being loud and disruptive.

- **Do not intrude on private property**

Trespassing on private property is punishable by fines or other penalties in Maui. Respect others' property and stay within designated public areas.

Maui safety recommendation

Here are some safety recommendations for Maui:

- **Keep an eye on the ocean's conditions**
Maui is famous for its beautiful beaches and crystal-clear waters, but the ocean can be dangerous if you are not cautious. Before venturing out, always check the ocean conditions and be aware of strong currents and rip tides. Never swim alone, and heed any warnings or advisories posted.

- **Sunscreen is essential**
Because Maui has a hot and sunny climate, it is critical to protect yourself from the sun's harmful rays. Wear high-SPF sunscreen and reapply it every few hours. Wear a hat and sunglasses, and seek shade during the hottest times of the day.

- **When hiking, exercise caution**

There are many beautiful hiking trails on Maui, but it's important to be cautious when hiking to avoid injury or becoming a loss. Always stay on designated trails and notify someone of your whereabouts and return time. Bring plenty of water and snacks, and dress comfortably.

- **When driving, use caution**

Maui has many scenic drives, but the roads can be narrow and winding, making driving difficult for some. Always drive defensively and within speed limits, and be aware of the island's unique driving conditions, such as steep hills and sharp curves. At night, be especially cautious because some roads may not be well-lit.

- **Keep your valuables secure**

Although Maui is a generally safe destination, it is still important to keep your valuables secure to avoid theft or loss. Cash, credit cards, and important documents should be kept in a safe, such as a hotel safe. Keep valuables out of your car and be cautious when using ATMs or making purchases.

- **Be cautious of wildlife**

Maui is home to many unique and beautiful wildlife species; however, it is critical to be aware of them and respect their habitat. Approaching or touching wildlife, as well as feeding them, can disrupt their natural behavior and be harmful to their health. Hiking in areas where bears or other potentially dangerous animals are known to live requires extra caution.

- **Understand the emergency phone numbers**

Before traveling to Maui, become acquainted with the local emergency phone numbers, such as police, fire, and medical services. It's critical to know who to call in an emergency and how to get help quickly.

Chapter 9: Understanding foreign transaction fees in Maui

When you purchase in a foreign country or a foreign currency, your bank or credit card company may charge you a foreign transaction fee. These fees are typically a percentage of the transaction amount and can quickly add up if you make numerous purchases.

If you use a credit or debit card issued by a bank outside the United States in Maui, you may be charged foreign transaction fees. These fees vary depending on your card issuer, but they usually range between 1% and 3% of the transaction amount.

You can avoid foreign transaction fees by using a credit or debit card that does not charge these fees in Maui. Some banks and credit card companies offer international travel cards with no foreign transaction fees. You can also avoid foreign transaction fees by using cash or traveler's checks instead of a credit card.

Before traveling to Maui, check with your bank or credit card company to understand their foreign transaction fee policies and to notify them that you will be traveling to avoid any card usage issues. Additionally, keep an eye on your account activity while in Maui to avoid being charged any unexpected fees.

Avoid phone roaming charges

Traveling to Maui is an exciting adventure, but you don't want to deal with unexpected cell phone roaming charges. While some cell phone companies offer international plans, they can be costly and have limited data allowances. Here are some pointers to help you avoid paying cell phone roaming fees while visiting Maui:

- **Whenever possible, use Wi-Fi**

Free Wi-Fi is available in many Maui restaurants, cafes, hotels, and tourist attractions. Use these options to connect to the internet without using up your cellular data plan. Download offline maps or use a map app that allows you to download maps ahead of time before visiting Maui.

- **Deactivate data roaming**

Before arriving in Maui, make sure to turn off data roaming on your phone. This will prevent your phone from connecting to a cellular network and incurring roaming charges. You can still connect to the internet and communicate with friends and family via Wi-Fi.

- **Purchase a SIM card from a local provider**

You can get a local SIM card in Maui if you have an unlocked phone. This allows you to use the network of a local carrier while avoiding international roaming fees. Local SIM cards are available at the airport and in local shops. Remember that you'll need to unlock your phone before you can use a local SIM card.

- **Invest in a travel SIM card**

If you don't want to buy a local SIM card, you can use a travel SIM card instead. Travel SIM cards are intended for international travelers and allow you to use the network of a local carrier without incurring roaming charges. These cards are available for purchase online or at certain retailers.

- **Use instant messaging apps**

Messaging apps such as WhatsApp, Facebook Messenger, and iMessage enable you to send text messages and make phone calls while connected to the internet. This means you won't have to use your cellular data plan to communicate with friends and family. To avoid unexpected charges, simply turn off cellular data for these apps.

- **Pre-download entertainment content**

Download your favorite movies, TV shows, and music to your phone or tablet before heading to Maui. You will be able to enjoy entertainment content without using your cellular data plan as a result of this. To keep yourself entertained on long flights or during downtime on your trip, you can also download e-books, podcasts, and other digital content.

- **Consider a Wi-Fi portable device**

Consider renting a portable Wi-Fi device if you need to stay connected while traveling. These devices function as Wi-Fi hotspots to which you can connect your phone, tablet, or laptop. You will be able to use the internet without using your cellular data plan as a result of this. Portable Wi-Fi access points can be rented at the airport or in local stores.

You can avoid unexpected cell phone roaming charges and stay connected while visiting Maui by following these tips. Before you travel, make sure to check with your cell phone provider to understand their international roaming policies and fees.

Utilization of the Maui mifi device and SIM card

If you're visiting Maui and need reliable internet access, a MiFi device and a local SIM card can be excellent options. This guide will go over how to use a MiFi device and SIM card in Maui, as well as the advantages of doing so.

What exactly is a MiFi?

A MiFi, also known as a mobile hotspot, is a small, portable device that lets you create a Wi-Fi network wherever you go. It functions by connecting to a cellular network and then broadcasting that connection as a Wi-Fi signal that you can access with your smartphone, tablet, or laptop. Many MiFi devices are small enough to fit in your pocket, making them convenient to travel with.

MiFi device usage in Maui

To use a MiFi device in Maui, you must first obtain a local SIM card from a local carrier. SIM cards are small, removable chips that are inserted into MiFi devices to activate them on the network of a specific carrier.

You can turn on the MiFi device after inserting a local SIM card. The device will then connect to the local cellular network and begin broadcasting a Wi-Fi signal that your devices can connect to.

The Advantages of Using a MiFi Device in Maui

There are several advantages to using a MiFi device and a local SIM card on Maui:

- Stay connected wherever you go: With a MiFi device, you can set up a Wi-Fi network anywhere in Maui. This means you can stay connected to the internet while on the move, whether you're at the beach, in a cafe, or exploring the island.

- Avoid costly data roaming charges from your home carrier by using a local SIM card with a MiFi device. Local SIM cards usually provide lower data usage rates than international roaming plans.

- Internet access that is faster and more reliable: A MiFi device can provide faster and more reliable internet access than public

Wi-Fi networks, which can be slow and unreliable in some areas of Maui.

- Share your internet connection with multiple devices: A MiFi device can connect multiple devices to the internet at the same time, allowing you to share your internet connection with friends or family members.

Where to get a MiFi device and a SIM card in Maui

Local carriers and electronics stores in Maui sell MiFi devices and SIM cards. AT&T, T-Mobile, and Verizon are among the most popular carriers in Maui. Rent a Satellite Phone or XCom Global can also provide you with a MiFi device.

Before purchasing a MiFi device and SIM card in Maui, make sure to research the various carriers and plans to find the best fit for your needs.

Consider coverage, data allowances, and rates when deciding on the best plan for you.

Advice on how to use a MiFi device and SIM card in Maui

Here are some pointers to help you make the most of your MiFi device and Maui SIM card:

- **Check coverage:** Before purchasing a local SIM card and MiFi device, research the carrier's coverage area. Some carriers may not have coverage in certain areas of Maui, so make sure you have a reliable connection wherever you go.

- **Monitor data usage:** Because local SIM cards may have data usage limits, it's critical to keep track of your usage to avoid surprises. Typically, you can monitor your data usage via the carrier's website or mobile app.

- **Keep the device charged:** Keep your MiFi device charged so you can use it when needed. Many devices have a battery life of several hours, but you should bring a portable charger or an extra battery pack just in case.

- **Protect your device:** A MiFi device, like any other electronic device, can be damaged by water, sand, and other environmental factors. When not in use, keep your device in a case or sleeve and avoid exposing it to water or other potential hazards.

- **Secure your connection**: When using a public Wi-Fi network, be wary of security risks such as hacking and identity theft. Use a strong password to protect your MiFi device and avoid accessing sensitive information or conducting financial transactions over public Wi-Fi networks.

Maui etiquette and customs

Customs and etiquette are important aspects of any culture, including Maui's. Understanding local customs and etiquette can help you navigate social situations more easily while also demonstrating respect for the local culture. In this guide, we'll go over some of the most important Maui customs and etiquette.

- **The Hawaiian Spirit**

The spirit of aloha is an important part of Hawaiian culture, and it can be found in many aspects of daily life on the island of Maui. Aloha, which can be translated as "love," "peace," or "compassion," represents a way of life that emphasizes kindness, generosity, and respect for others.

Visitors to Maui are encouraged to embrace the spirit of aloha by being kind and respectful to others and by appreciating the island's natural beauty and culture.

- **Regards and salutations**

It is customary in Maui to greet others with a friendly "aloha" and a smile. It is customary to exchange a lei, a traditional Hawaiian flower garland, as a sign of welcome and respect when meeting someone for the first time.

When visiting a sacred site or attending a cultural event, it is important to dress appropriately, follow any rules or guidelines, and avoid any disrespectful or disruptive behavior.

- **Punctuality**

Punctuality is valued in Maui, and being late for a meeting or event is considered impolite. If you are late, communicate with the other party and apologize for any inconvenience.

- **Gift-Giving**

Gift-giving is an important part of Hawaiian culture, and it is commonly used to express gratitude and strengthen relationships. It is customary to bring a small gift for your hosts, such as a box of chocolates, a bottle of wine, or a locally made souvenir when visiting Maui.

- **Dress code**

In most situations, shorts, t-shirts, and sandals are acceptable attire. However, when visiting certain places, such as restaurants, it is important to dress appropriately and avoid wearing beachwear or clothing that is too revealing.

- **Tipping**

Tipping is common in Maui, and it is customary to tip between 15-20% for excellent service in restaurants, bars, and other service industries. Housekeepers and tour guides are also commonly tipped.

- **Beach Protocol**

Maui's beaches are among the most beautiful in the world, and it is critical that they and the people who use them be respected. It is critical to follow any posted rules and guidelines, as well as to respect the privacy and space of others when visiting the beach.

It is also critical to avoid littering and properly dispose of trash. It is critical to avoid touching or harming any marine life while snorkeling or swimming and to be aware of any potential hazards such as strong currents or sharp coral.

- **Nature is to be respected**

Maui's natural beauty is one of the island's most valuable resources, and it is critical to respect the environment and help preserve it for future generations. It is critical to stay on designated paths when hiking or exploring nature trails to avoid damaging any vegetation or wildlife.

It is also critical to avoid littering and properly dispose of trash, as well as to consider any potential environmental consequences of your actions.

- **The local community should be respected**

Maui's community is vibrant and diverse, and it is important to respect the local culture and traditions. When visiting Maui, it is critical to learn about local customs and be aware of any cultural differences or taboos.

It is also critical to avoid any disrespectful or offensive behavior and to be aware of the impact of your actions on the local community. For example, when attending events or visiting sacred sites, it is critical to avoid loud or disruptive behavior in residential areas, as well as to respect any local customs or traditions.

- **Language**

Hawaii's official languages are English and Hawaiian, but many locals also speak Japanese, Tagalog, and Chinese. When visiting Maui, it's a good idea to know a few basic Hawaiian phrases like "mahalo" (thank you) and "aloha" (hello/goodbye).

When communicating with locals who may not speak English fluently, it is also important to be aware of any language barriers and to use clear and simple language.

Making new friends on Maui

Making friends in Maui can be a fantastic way to enhance your island experience. There are numerous opportunities to meet new people and form long-lasting connections in Maui, whether you are visiting for a short vacation or living there permanently.

In this guide, we'll go over some strategies for making friends on Maui, as well as some activities and groups that can help you connect with others on the island.

- **Accept the Spirit of Aloha**

The spirit of aloha is an important part of Hawaiian culture, and it can be an effective tool for making new friends in Maui. Adopting the aloha spirit entails treating others with kindness, respect, and compassion, as well as approaching social situations with an open and positive attitude.

By embodying the spirit of aloha, you can create a welcoming and friendly environment that is conducive to meeting new people and forming long-lasting relationships.

- **Participate in Community Events**

Maui has a thriving and diverse community, and there are numerous events and activities available to help you meet new people and connect with others who share your interests.

Whether you like music, art, sports, or food, Maui has events and festivals all year that celebrate the island's unique culture and traditions. Attending these events can be a great way to meet new people and converse with others who share your interests.

- **Join Local Organizations**

There are numerous local groups and organizations in Maui that cater to a wide range of interests and activities. There are numerous opportunities to connect with others who share your interests and passions, from hiking and surfing groups to book clubs and community service organizations.

Joining a local group or organization can be a wonderful way to meet new people and form long-lasting friendships. It may also provide opportunities for you to give back to the community and have a positive impact on Maui.

- **Volunteer**

Volunteering is a fantastic way to meet new people while also contributing to the community. On Maui, many organizations rely on volunteers to help with everything from beach cleanups and animal rescue to mentoring and tutoring.

Volunteering can be a rewarding and fulfilling experience, as well as a way to connect with others who share your desire to help others and make a positive difference in the community.

- **Participate in Classes or Workshops**

Maui is home to many talented artists, musicians, and craftspeople, and there are a variety of classes and workshops available to help you learn new skills and connect with others who share your interests.

There are classes and workshops available for a wide range of interests and skill levels, whether you want to learn how to play the ukulele, paint a watercolor, or make traditional Hawaiian crafts.

- **Take Action**

Maui is known for its natural beauty and outdoor activities, and getting out and about can be a great way to meet new people and form long-lasting friendships. There are many opportunities to get active and connect with others who share your passion, whether you enjoy hiking, surfing, yoga, or any other outdoor activity.

Joining a local sports team or fitness group can be an excellent way to meet new people and stay active while exploring Maui's stunning natural surroundings.

Chapter 10: Travelling with family in Maui

Travelling with family is always a great way to create lifelong memories, and Maui is one of the most beautiful destinations in the world to do so. Known as the Valley Isle, Maui is the second-largest island in Hawaii and offers a plethora of activities and attractions that are perfect for families.

Maui is a paradise with beautiful beaches, lush forests, and breathtaking landscapes. Whether you're looking to relax on the beach, go on an adventure, or experience Hawaiian culture, Maui has something for everyone.

When travelling with family in Maui, one of the first things to consider is accommodations. Maui has a variety of options, including hotels, resorts, vacation rentals, and condos. Many resorts offer amenities such as swimming pools, hot tubs, and kid-friendly activities. Vacation rentals and condos are also great options for families, as they often come with a full kitchen, multiple bedrooms, and a living room, which provides more space and flexibility for families.

The next thing to consider when planning a family trip to Maui is transportation. Maui has several transportation options, including rental cars, taxis, ride-sharing services, and public transportation. Rental cars are an excellent option for families, as they provide more flexibility and allow you to explore the island at your own pace. If you plan on doing a lot of driving, it's essential to book a rental car in advance, as they can be in high demand during peak travel seasons.

One of the best things about Maui is its beautiful beaches. Maui has over 30 miles of beautiful coastline, and each beach has its own unique charm. Some of the best family-friendly beaches in Maui include Kaanapali Beach, Napili Beach, and

Kapalua Beach. These beaches offer calm waters, soft sand, and plenty of activities such as snorkeling, paddleboarding, and beach volleyball.

Another great activity for families in Maui is exploring the island's natural wonders. Maui is home to several incredible waterfalls, including the famous Road to Hana, which features dozens of waterfalls along the way. Families can take a guided tour or rent a car and explore on their own. Some other popular natural attractions include Haleakala National Park, which features a stunning volcanic crater, and Iao Valley State Park, which offers lush forests and scenic hiking trails.

For families looking to experience Hawaiian culture, Maui has several options as well. One popular cultural activity is attending a traditional Hawaiian luau. These events feature hula dancers, fire knife performances, and traditional Hawaiian cuisine. Families can also visit historical sites such as the Lahaina Historic Trail, which showcases Maui's rich history and culture.

Another great activity for families in Maui is whale watching. During the winter months, humpback whales migrate to Maui's waters to mate and give birth. Several companies offer whale watching tours, which provide an up-close look at these magnificent creatures.

Finally, no trip to Maui would be complete without trying the island's delicious food. Hawaiian cuisine is a fusion of several different cultures, including Japanese, Chinese, Filipino, and Portuguese. Some popular dishes to try include poke, a raw fish salad, loco moco, a rice and meat dish, and shaved ice, a Hawaiian dessert made with ice and flavored syrup.

Holiday activities for family in Maui

Maui is a perfect holiday destination for families looking for a mix of relaxation and adventure. The island offers a wide range of activities for all ages, making it an ideal destination for families with children. Here are some of the top holiday activities for families in Maui:

- **Whale Watching**

Whale watching is a popular activity in Maui, and the best time to do it is from December to April when humpback whales migrate to Maui's waters to mate and give birth. Several companies offer whale watching tours, which provide an up-close look at these magnificent creatures.

- **Snorkeling**

Maui has some of the best snorkeling spots in Hawaii, and exploring the island's underwater world is a must-do activity for families. Snorkeling in Molokini Crater, located just off the coast of Maui, is a unique experience that families will never forget.

- **Road to Hana**

The Road to Hana is a scenic drive that takes you through Maui's lush rainforest, past waterfalls, and along the coast. This drive is a great way to explore the island's natural beauty, and there are plenty of opportunities to stop and take in the sights along the way.

- **Haleakala National Park**

Haleakala National Park is a must-visit for families in Maui. The park features a stunning volcanic crater and offers scenic hiking trails, ranger-led programs, and stargazing opportunities.

- **Hawaiian Luau**

A Hawaiian Luau is a traditional Hawaiian party that features hula dancers, fire knife performances, and traditional Hawaiian cuisine. Attending a luau is a great way to experience Hawaiian culture and entertainment.

- **Surfing and Stand-Up Paddleboarding**

Maui is a surfer's paradise, and learning to surf or stand-up paddleboard is a fun activity for families. There are several surfing schools and rental shops that offer lessons and equipment.

- **Ziplining**

Ziplining is an exciting activity that allows families to see Maui's natural beauty from a unique perspective. There are several zipline courses on the island, and most offer family-friendly options.

- **Maui Ocean Center**

The Maui Ocean Center is a must-visit attraction for families in Maui. The center features over 60 exhibits and thousands of marine animals, including sharks, sea turtles, and stingrays.

- **ATV Tours**

Taking an ATV tour is a thrilling way to explore Maui's backcountry. These tours take you through the island's rugged terrain and offer stunning views of the ocean and mountains.

Traveling with children to Maui

Traveling with children can be challenging, but a family vacation to Maui can be an exciting adventure for all. Maui is a tropical paradise with beautiful beaches, lush landscapes, and fun activities for people of all ages. You can make your family vacation a memorable and enjoyable experience with proper planning and preparation. In this guide, we will give you some advice and suggestions for traveling to Maui with children.

- **Choose an appropriate time to travel**

When traveling with children, choosing the best time to travel is critical. The peak season in Maui lasts from mid-December to mid-April, and prices are generally higher. Summer months are also busy and may be more expensive due to school holidays. The best time to visit Maui with kids is in the spring or fall when the weather is nice and crowds are smaller. Furthermore, during these times, you may be able to find some excellent deals on lodging and activities.

- **Make a plan ahead of time**

When traveling with children, planning is essential. Make a travel itinerary that includes all of the destinations and activities you want to do. When planning activities for your children, keep their age and interests in mind. Make time in your schedule for everyone to rest and recharge. You can also look for family-friendly hotels and resorts with amenities like kid's clubs, swimming pools, and babysitting services.

- **Pack wisely**

When traveling with children, proper packing is essential. Make a packing list for each member of the family, including necessities such as sunscreen, hats, swimwear, and comfortable shoes. Pack snacks and drinks for the plane ride and day trips. You might also want to bring some entertainment for the kids, such as books, games, and tablets, to keep them entertained during the trip.

- **Renting a car is an option**

Maui is a small island, but it has a lot to offer. Renting a car allows you to explore the island at your own pace while avoiding the inconvenience of public transportation. You can also rent car seats for your children if you prefer not to bring your own. However, keep in mind that driving in Maui can be difficult, especially if you are unfamiliar with driving on narrow, winding roads.

- **Visit beaches that are suitable for children**

Maui is well-known for its beautiful beaches, and there are numerous family-friendly activities available. Ka'anapali Beach, Kapalua Beach, and Napili Beach are some of the best beaches for families. These beaches are ideal for swimming, snorkeling, and building sandcastles because of their calm waters and sandy shores. Check out the lifeguard stations and follow their instructions to ensure the safety of your family.

- **Hike with the family**

Many beautiful trails on Maui are appropriate for families with children. The Kapalua Coastal Trail, which offers stunning views of the ocean and lush landscapes, is a popular choice. Iao Valley State Park, with its scenic trails and historic sites, is another excellent option. Pack plenty of water and snacks for your hike, and dress comfortably.

- **Learn about the local culture**

Maui has a rich cultural heritage that children can learn from. The Maui Arts and Cultural Center hosts exhibits, workshops, and performances that highlight Hawaiian culture. You can also enjoy Hawaiian music, dance, and food at a traditional luau. You can also go to Haleakala National Park, which has breathtaking scenery and historic sites.

- **Taste the local cuisine**

Maui is a foodie's paradise, with a plethora of restaurants and food trucks serving up delectable local fare. Traditional Hawaiian dishes such as poke, kalua pig, and shaved ice are available. There are also numerous farmers' markets where you can sample local fruits and vegetables. Introducing children to local cuisine is a fun way to introduce them to new flavors and cultures.

- **Engage in water sports**

Maui is well-known for its water sports, and there are numerous activities for kids. Snorkeling is a popular activity, and many snorkeling tours provide opportunities to see marine life up close. You can also take lessons in paddleboarding, kayaking, and surfing. Check the age and weight restrictions for each activity, and go with a reputable company that prioritizes safety.

- **Make use of kids' clubs**

Many Maui hotels and resorts offer children's clubs and programs that provide activities and entertainment. These programs are typically tailored to various age groups and may include games, crafts, and outdoor activities. This can provide parents with much-needed time to unwind and participate in adult activities.

Top Maui family activities

Maui is an excellent destination for families with children, as there are numerous fun activities for kids of all ages. This guide will discuss the top ten kids' activities in Maui, as well as how to get there.

- **Snorkeling**

Snorkeling is a popular activity in Maui, and it's a great way for kids to learn about the ocean. Molokini Crater, Honolua Bay, and Black Rock are among the best snorkeling spots in Maui. Most snorkeling tours include equipment rental and guides to assist you and your children in safely navigating the waters. You can take a tour or rent a car and drive to these snorkeling spots.

- **Surfing**

Surfing is an enjoyable activity for children who enjoy being in the water and want to try something new. Lahaina, Kihei, and Kalama Beach are among the best beginner surf spots on Maui. Many surf schools offer lessons for children, and the instructors are well-trained to ensure a fun and safe experience. You can rent a car or use a shuttle service to get to the surf spots.

- **National Park of Haleakala**

Haleakala National Park is a stunning destination for outdoor-loving families. The park contains beautiful scenery, hiking trails, and historic sites. The Haleakala Crater is a must-see attraction that provides a once-in-a-lifetime opportunity to explore a dormant volcano. You can drive to the park entrance or take a guided tour to get to Haleakala National Park.

- **Maui Ocean Center**

The Maui Ocean Center is a fantastic place to learn about marine life and get up close and personal with sea creatures. The center has a shark tank, turtle lagoon, and touch pool, among other exhibits and interactive displays. You can drive to the Maui Ocean Center or take a shuttle from your hotel.

- **Ziplining**

Ziplining is an exciting activity for adventurous children. Maui has several zipline courses, such as Skyline Eco-Adventures, where you can zip through the trees while admiring the island's stunning views. Most zipline companies provide equipment and guides, and most allow children to participate. You can rent a car or use a shuttle service to get to the zipline course.

- **Plantation on Maui**

The Maui Tropical Plantation is a lovely destination for families interested in learning about the flora and fauna of the island. There are guided tours, tram rides, and a zipline course at the plantation. Children can learn about various plants and animals while also enjoying the stunning scenery. You can drive or take a shuttle service to the Maui Tropical Plantation.

- **The Submarine Atlantis**

The Atlantis Submarine is a one-of-a-kind way to see the underwater world without getting wet. The submarine transports you to the ocean floor, where you can see marine life and shipwrecks. The thrill of being inside a submarine and seeing the ocean up close will appeal to children. You can either drive or take a shuttle to the Atlantis Submarine.

- **Yoga with goats on Maui**

Maui Goat Yoga is a unique and enjoyable activity for children who enjoy animals. The class is held on a farm where participants can practice yoga while playing with baby goats. The goats are friendly and playful, and the class is appropriate for participants of all skill levels. You can rent a car or schedule a shuttle service to get to Maui Goat Yoga.

- **Ocean Riders from Maui**

Maui Ocean Riders provide ocean rafting, snorkeling, and whale-watching tours. The tours are led by knowledgeable guides who are well-versed in marine life on Maui. Children will enjoy the excitement of riding on a fast boat and getting up close and personal with whales, dolphins, and other sea creatures. You can drive yourself or take a shuttle to Maui Ocean Riders.

- **Beaches**

Maui has some of the world's most beautiful beaches, and it's a must-see destination for families with children. Kaanapali Beach, Napili Bay, and Wailea Beach are some of the best beaches for families. Children can enjoy sandcastle building, swimming in the ocean, and other beach activities. You can either rent a car or take a shuttle service to the beaches.

Children's safety in Maui

When planning a family vacation in Maui, it is critical to consider child safety precautions. The island has a wide range of outdoor activities, which can be enjoyable but also dangerous. Here are some safety tips to keep in mind when visiting Maui with children.

- **Sun protection is essential**

Maui is known for its beautiful weather, but the sun can be harsh. Sun protection is particularly important for children. Make sure your kids have plenty of sunscreen, hats, and sunglasses. It's also important to avoid the sun between 10 a.m. and 4 p.m. and to seek shade whenever possible.

- **Water security**

Although Maui has many beautiful beaches and water activities, you must take precautions to keep your children safe. Always keep an eye on your children and teach them to swim if they don't know how. Before swimming or participating in water activities, it is also critical to understand the ocean conditions. Strong currents, high surf, and jellyfish can all be dangerous, so check for warnings and advisories at all times.

- **Wildlife**

Wildlife on Maui includes sea turtles and whales. While seeing these creatures up close is exciting, it is critical to remember to respect their space and habitat. When viewing wildlife, never touch or disturb it, and keep a safe distance from it.

- **Driving**

If you intend to explore Maui by car, you must practice safe driving habits. The island's roads are narrow and winding, making navigation difficult, especially for those who are not used to driving on the right side of the road. Wear your seatbelts and obey speed limits and traffic signs. It's also crucial to avoid distractions while driving, such as using your phone.

- **Hiking and other outdoor pursuits**

Some of the most beautiful hiking trails and outdoor activities in the world can be found in Maui. However, before engaging in these activities, it is critical to be prepared and to take the necessary precautions. Make sure you research the trail or activity ahead of time and understand the level of difficulty. Bring plenty of water, snacks, and a first-aid kit with you at all times. It is also critical to dress appropriately and be aware of the weather conditions.

- **The safety of food and water**

Maui has a plethora of delicious food options, but it's critical to keep food and water safety in mind, especially for children. Avoid drinking tap water, ice, and uncooked food from street vendors. It is also essential to wash your hands frequently and to use hand sanitizer as needed.

Frequently Asked Questions

- **When should you go to Maui?**

The months of April to May and September to November are ideal for a visit to Maui. These months provide pleasant weather, fewer visitors, and lower prices.

- **What are the top Maui attractions?**

The Road to Hana, Haleakala National Park, Iao Valley State Park, Lahaina, and the beaches are among the must-see attractions on Maui.

- **Which are the best Maui beaches?**

Kaanapali Beach, Wailea Beach, Napili Bay, and Makena Beach are among the best beaches in Maui.

- **What exactly is the Hana Highway?**

The Road to Hana is a scenic drive along Maui's east coast, known for its beautiful waterfalls, lush vegetation, and beaches.

- **What is the purpose of Haleakala National Park?**

Haleakala National Park is a national park on the Hawaiian island of Maui that is famous for its spectacular sunrises and sunsets, hiking trails, and unique volcanic landscape.

- **What is the weather in Maui like?**

Throughout the year, the weather in Maui is warm and tropical, with average temperatures ranging from 70 to 85 degrees Fahrenheit.

- **What are some Maui outdoor activities?**

Snorkeling, surfing, hiking, whale watching, and zip-lining are just a few of the outdoor activities available on Maui.

- **How is the food in Maui?**

Hawaiian, Japanese, and other Asian cuisines have influenced Maui's cuisine. Poke, spam musubi, and loco moco are all popular local dishes.

- **What is Maui nightlife like?**

Maui's nightlife is modest, with many bars and restaurants closing early. There are, however, a few places where you can hear live music and dance.

- **How should I get around Maui?**

Because public transportation is limited in Maui, driving is the best way to get around. Renting a car or going on a tour are both viable options.

- **Is Maui a good place for families?**

Yes, Maui is a family-friendly destination with plenty of activities and attractions for kids and families.

- **What does it cost to live in Maui?**

Housing, food, and transportation are among the more expensive expenses in Maui, which is higher than the national average.

- **What is the official language of Maui?**

While English is the official language of Maui, Hawaiian, and other Polynesian languages are also spoken.

- **Is there any culture in Maui?**

Yes, there are many cultural events in Maui throughout the year, such as hula festivals, lei-making workshops, and Hawaiian music concerts.

- **What's it like to shop in Maui?**

Maui's shopping options range from high-end boutiques to local artisan markets.

Conclusion

Maui is a fantastic tourist destination with a diverse range of experiences. Maui has something for everyone, from its breathtaking beaches and waterfalls to its rich cultural heritage and exciting outdoor activities. This travel guide has provided a thorough overview of the island, highlighting some of its must-see attractions, top-rated accommodations, and best dining options.

Maui offers a variety of relaxing beach vacation options, including the iconic Kaanapali Beach, Wailea Beach, and Napili Bay. Each beach has its distinct features and atmosphere, giving visitors a variety of options to suit their tastes. Maui's beaches have something for everyone, whether you enjoy sunbathing, swimming, snorkeling, or surfing.

Maui is also well-known for its stunning waterfalls, such as the iconic Road to Hana, which is a must-see for anyone visiting the island. Furthermore, the island's lush rainforests and hiking trails provide outdoor enthusiasts with numerous opportunities to explore and connect with nature.

Visitors are drawn to the island's rich cultural heritage, which includes numerous historic sites and cultural centers that provide a glimpse into Hawaii's fascinating past. Among the many cultural attractions on the island are the Lahaina Historic District, Haleakala National Park, and the Hana Cultural Center.

Maui has a variety of lodging options to suit all budgets and preferences. Visitors can choose between luxury resorts, affordable hotels, and cozy vacation rentals, all of which provide excellent service and amenities.

Finally, Maui is well-known for its diverse cuisine, with a variety of international and local eateries to choose from. Traditional Hawaiian dishes like poi and poke, as well as international favorites like sushi and Thai curries, are available to visitors. Maui has something for everyone's culinary tastes.

Hello, I hope you got value from this guide. I'm Sarah k. Cox, I research and write books about travel guides to help my readers have the best experience possible while traveling around the world. To continue satisfying and providing value to you, I must improve my content and research processes. I can only get better with your help. As a result, I'd appreciate your feedback. Thank you very much.

Made in the USA
Las Vegas, NV
07 December 2023

82265464R00120